T0238742

REST API Development with Node.js

Manage and Understand the Full Capabilities of Successful REST Development

Second Edition

Fernando Doglio

Apress®

REST API Development with Node.js

Fernando Doglio
La Paz, Canelones, Uruguay

ISBN-13 (pbk): 978-1-4842-3714-4 ISBN-13 (electronic): 978-1-4842-3715-1
https://doi.org/10.1007/978-1-4842-3715-1

Library of Congress Control Number: 2018950838

Copyright © 2018 by Fernando Doglio

This work is subject to copyright. All rights are reserved by the Publisher, whether the whole or part of the material is concerned, specifically the rights of translation, reprinting, reuse of illustrations, recitation, broadcasting, reproduction on microfilms or in any other physical way, and transmission or information storage and retrieval, electronic adaptation, computer software, or by similar or dissimilar methodology now known or hereafter developed.

Trademarked names, logos, and images may appear in this book. Rather than use a trademark symbol with every occurrence of a trademarked name, logo, or image we use the names, logos, and images only in an editorial fashion and to the benefit of the trademark owner, with no intention of infringement of the trademark.

The use in this publication of trade names, trademarks, service marks, and similar terms, even if they are not identified as such, is not to be taken as an expression of opinion as to whether or not they are subject to proprietary rights.

While the advice and information in this book are believed to be true and accurate at the date of publication, neither the authors nor the editors nor the publisher can accept any legal responsibility for any errors or omissions that may be made. The publisher makes no warranty, express or implied, with respect to the material contained herein.

Managing Director, Apress Media LLC: Welmoed Spahr
Acquisitions Editor: Louise Corrigan
Development Editor: James Markham
Coordinating Editor: Nancy Chen

Cover designed by eStudioCalamar

Cover image designed by Freepik (www.freepik.com)

Distributed to the book trade worldwide by Springer Science+Business Media New York, 233 Spring Street, 6th Floor, New York, NY 10013. Phone 1-800-SPRINGER, fax (201) 348-4505, e-mail orders-ny@springer-sbm.com, or visit www.springeronline.com. Apress Media, LLC is a California LLC and the sole member (owner) is Springer Science + Business Media Finance Inc (SSBM Finance Inc). SSBM Finance Inc is a **Delaware** corporation.

For information on translations, please e-mail rights@apress.com, or visit http://www.apress.com/rights-permissions.

Apress titles may be purchased in bulk for academic, corporate, or promotional use. eBook versions and licenses are also available for most titles. For more information, reference our Print and eBook Bulk Sales web page at http://www.apress.com/bulk-sales.

Any source code or other supplementary material referenced by the author in this book is available to readers on GitHub via the book's product page, located at www.apress.com/9781484237144. For more detailed information, please visit http://www.apress.com/source-code.

Printed on acid-free paper

To my loving wife, without whom this book would've never happened and to my beautiful boys, without whom this book would've happened a lot sooner...

Thank you!

Table of Contents

About the Author

Fernando Doglio has worked as a developer for the past 13 years. In that time, he has come to love the Web and has had the opportunity to work with most leading technologies, such as PHP, Ruby on Rails, MySQL, Node.js, Angular.js, AJAX, REST APIs, and others. For the past 4 years Fernando has also been working as a Technical Manager and Technical Lead for BigData projects.

In his spare time, Fernando likes to tinker, learn new things, and write technical articles and books such as this one. He's also a big open source supporter, always trying to bring new people into that realm. When not programming, he is spending time with his family.

Fernando can be contacted on Twitter @deleteman123 or online at www.fernandodoglio.com.

About the Technical Reviewer

Takashi Mukoda is an international student at Purchase College/State University of New York. Now, he is taking a semester off and is back home in Japan. At Purchase College, he majors in Mathematics/Computer Science and New Media and has worked as a teaching assistant for computing and mathematics courses.

Takashi likes playing the keyboard and going on hikes in mountains to take pictures. His interest in programming and art incites him to create multi-media art pieces. Some of them are built with Processing and interact with human motion and sounds.

(Website: http://www.takashimukoda.com)

Acknowledgments

I'd like to thank the amazing technical reviewer involved in the project, Takashi Mukoda, whose great feedback was a crucial contribution to the making of this book.

I'd also like to thank the rest of the Apress editorial team, whose guidance helped me through the process of writing this, my first book.

Introduction

These days, everyone is finding a new way to interconnect systems; the Internet of Things (IoT), for instance, is the new kid on the block, but who knows what will come later.

The point is that in order to interconnect systems, as an architect, you're better off using standard methods that allow for a faster adoption of your technology. In particular, APIs allow for the creation of standards and can work under known and well-tested core technologies like HTTP.

If you add to that a well-defined style guide like REST, you've got yourself the means to create a scalable, technology-agnostic, and uniform interface for your services to be consumed by your clients.

Welcome to *REST API Development with Node.js*. This book will cover REST, API development, and, finally, how these two mix up with Node.js.

Starting from a theoretical point of view, you'll learn how REST came to be, who created it, and its characteristics. Later, you'll move toward the practical side by going over API development and the lessons that years of experience from the community have taught us. Finally, you'll move into a fully practical approach, and you'll see how Node.js and its modules can help create a RESTful API. You'll also get a taste of what a real-world development flow would be like and what it would take to both test and deploy your code into a production environment.

The final chapters will be 100% practical, going over a real-world example of a RESTful API developed in Node.js. I will cover everything from the requirement-gathering process, to tools selection, through actual development, and, finally, you'll land in troubleshooting-land, where I'll discuss the different things that can go wrong and how to tackle them.

Now sit back, relax, and enjoy the reading.

CHAPTER 1

REST 101

Nowadays, the acronym REST has become a buzzword, and as such, it's being thrown into the digital wind very carelessly by a lot of tech people without fully understanding what it really means. Just because you can interact with a system using HTTP, and send JSON back and forth, doesn't mean it's a RESTful system. REST is a lot more than that—and that is what we'll cover in this chapter.

Let's start where it all began, with Roy Fielding's paper, going over the main characteristics of his idea. I'll try to explain the main aspects of it, the constraints he added, and why he added them. I'll go over some examples and then jump backward into the past, because even though REST has proven to be a huge jump forward regarding distributed systems interconnection, before Fielding's paper became popular, developers were still looking for solutions to the problem: how to easily interconnect a nonhomogeneous set of systems.

I'll do a quick review of the options developers had back then to interconnect systems, mainly going over SOAP and XML-RPC (the two main players before REST).

In the end, I'll jump back to our current time, comparing the advantages that REST brought us and thus showing why is it so popular today.

But first, a small clarification is in order: As you'll read in just a few minutes, REST is *protocol-independent* (as long as the protocol has support for a URI scheme), but for the sake of this book and since we're focusing on API design, let's assume that the protocol we're using is HTTP, which will simplify explanations and examples. And as long as you keep in mind that the same is true for other protocols (like FTP), then you'll be fine.

© Fernando Doglio 2018
F. Doglio, *REST API Development with Node.js*, https://doi.org/10.1007/978-1-4842-3715-1_1

Where Did It All Start?

This whole thing started with Roy Fielding, an American computer scientist born in 1965. He is one of the main authors of the HTTP protocol[1] (the protocol upon which the entire Web infrastructure is based). He is also one of the co-authors of the Apache Web server[2] and he was the chair of the Apache Software Foundation[3] for the first 3 years of its existence.

So, as you can see, Fielding has made a lot of great contributions to the IT world, especially regarding the Internet, but I think that his doctoral thesis is the thing that received the most attention and made his name known among a lot of people who otherwise wouldn't have heard of him.

In the year 2000, Fielding presented his doctoral dissertation, *Architectural Styles and the Design of Network-based Software Architecture*[4]. In it he coined the term *REST*, an architectural style for distributed hypermedia systems.

Put simply, REST (short for *REpresentational State Transfer*) is an architectural style defined to help create and organize distributed systems. The key word from that definition should be *style*, because an important aspect of REST (which is one of the main reasons books like this one exist) is that it is an architectural style—not a guideline, not a standard, nor anything that would imply that there are a set of hard rules to follow to end up having a RESTful architecture.

And because it is a style, and there is no Request for Comments (RFC) out there to define it, it's subject to misinterpretations from the people reading about it. Not only that, but some go as far as to leave parts out and implement a subset of its features, which in turn leads to a widespread and incomplete REST ideal, leaving out features that would otherwise be useful and help your system's users.

The main idea behind REST is that a distributed system, organized RESTfully, will improve in the following areas:

- *Performance*: The communication style proposed by REST is meant to be efficient and simple, allowing a performance boost on systems that adopt it.

---

[1]See https://www.ietf.org/rfc/rfc2616.txt.

[2]See http://httpd.apache.org/.

[3]See http://www.apache.org/.

[4]See http://www.ics.uci.edu/~fielding/pubs/dissertation/rest_arch_style.htm.

- *Scalability of component interaction*: Any distributed system should be able to handle this aspect well enough, and the simple interaction proposed by REST greatly allows for this.

- *Simplicity of interface*: A simple interface allows for simpler interactions between systems, which in turn can grant benefits like the ones previously mentioned.

- *Modifiability of components*: The distributed nature of the system, and the separation of concerns proposed by REST (more on this in a bit), allows for components to be modified independently of each other at a minimum cost and risk.

- *Portability*: REST is technology- and language-agnostic, meaning that it can be implemented and consumed by any type of technology (there are some constraints that I'll go over in a bit, but no specific technology is enforced).

- *Reliability*: The stateless constraint proposed by REST (more on this later) allows for the easier recovery of a system after failure.

- *Visibility*: Again, the stateless constraint proposed has the added benefit of improving visibility, because any monitoring system doesn't need to look further than a single request message to determine the full state of said request (this will become clear once I talk about the constraints in a bit).

From this list, some direct benefits can be extrapolated.

- A component-centric design allows you to make systems that are very fault tolerant. Having the failure of one component not affect the entire stability of the system is a great benefit for any system.

- Interconnecting components is quite easy, minimizing the risks when adding new features or scaling up or down.

- A system designed with REST in mind will be accessible to a wider audience, thanks to its portability (as described earlier).With a generic interface, the system can be used by a wider range of developers.

To achieve these properties and benefits, a set of constraints were added to REST to help define a uniform connector interface.

REST Constraints

According to Fielding, there are two ways to define a system. One approach is to start from a blank slate, an empty whiteboard, with no initial knowledge of the system being built or the use of familiar components until the needs are satisfied. A second approach is to start with the full set of needs for the system, and constraints are added to individual components until the forces that influence the system are able to interact in harmony with each other.

REST follows the second approach. To define a REST architecture, a null-state is initially defined—a system that has no constraints whatsoever and where component differentiation is nothing but a myth—and constraints are added one by one.

Client–Server

The first constraint to be added is one of the most common ones on network-based architectures: *client–server*. A server is in charge of handling a set of services, and it listens for requests regarding said services. The requests, in turn, are made via a connector by a client system needing one of those services (see Figure 1-1).

The main principle behind this constraint is the *separation of concerns*. It allows for the separation of front-end code (representation and possible UI-related processing of the information) from the server-side code, which should take care of storage and server-side processing of the data.

This constraint allows for the independent evolution of both components, offering a great deal of flexibility by letting client applications improve without affecting the server code and vice-versa.

Figure 1-1. *Client–Server architecture diagram*

Stateless

The constraint to be added on top of the previous one is the *stateless* constraint (see Figure 1-2). Communication between client and·server must be stateless, meaning that each request done from the client must have all the information required for the server to understand it, without taking advantage of any stored data.

This constraint represents several improvements for the underlying architecture:

- *Visibility*: Monitoring the system becomes easy when all the information required is inside the request.

- *Scalability*: By not having to store data between requests, the server can free resources faster.

- *Reliability*: As mentioned earlier, a system that is stateless can recover from a failure much easier than one that isn't, since the only thing to recover is the application itself.

- *Easier implementation*: Writing code that doesn't have to manage stored-state data across multiple servers is much easier to do, thus the full server-side system becomes simpler.

Although at first glance this constraint might seem nothing but good, as what normally happens, there is a trade-off. On one hand, benefits are gained by the system, but on the other side, network traffic could potentially be harmed by adding a minor overhead on every request from sending repeated state information. Depending on the type of system being implemented, and the amount of repeated information, this might not be an acceptable trade-off.

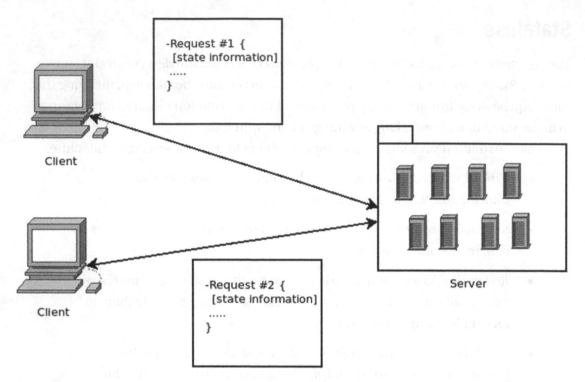

Figure 1-2. *Representation of the stateless constraint*

Cacheable

The *cacheable* constraint is added to the current set of constraints (see Figure 1-3). It proposes that every response to a request must be explicitly or implicitly set as cacheable (when applicable).

By caching the responses, there are some obvious benefits that get added to the architecture: on the server side, some interactions (a database request, for example) are completely bypassed while the content is cached. On the client side, an apparent improvement of performance is perceived.

The trade-off with this constraint is the possibility of cached data being stale, due to poor caching rules. This constraint is, again, dependent on the type of system being implemented.

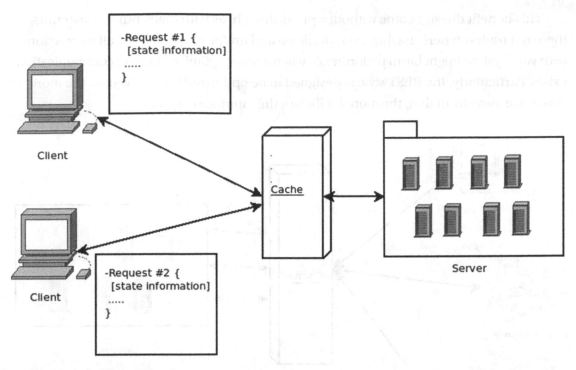

Figure 1-3. *Representation of a client-stateless-cache-server architecture*

Note   Figure 1-3 shows the cache as an external layer between the clients and the servers. This is only one possible implementation of it. The cache layer could be living inside the client (i.e., browser cache) or inside the servers themselves.

Uniform Interface

One of REST's main characteristics and winning points when compared to other alternatives is the *uniform interface* constraint. By keeping a uniform interface between components, you simplify the job of the client when it comes to interacting with your system (see Figure 1-4). Another major winning point here is that the client's implementation is independent of yours, so by defining a standard and uniform interface for all of your services, you effectively simplified the implementation of independent clients by giving them a clear set of rules to follow.

Said rules are not part of the REST style, but there are constraints that can be used to create such rules for each individual case.

This benefit doesn't come without a price, though; as with many other constraints, there is a trade-off here: having a standardized and uniform interface for all interactions with your system might harm performance when a more optimized form of communication exists. Particularly, the REST style is designed to be optimized for the Web, so the more you move away from that, the more inefficient the interface can be.

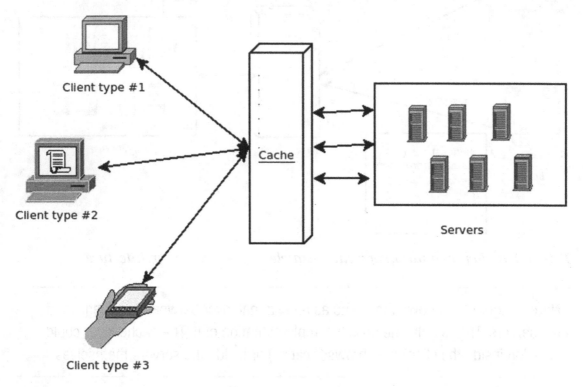

Figure 1-4. *Different client types can interact seamlessly with servers thanks to the uniform interface*

Note   To achieve the uniform interface, a new set of constraints must be added to the interface: identification of resources, manipulation of resources through representation, self-descriptive messages, and hypermedia as the engine of application state (a.k.a. HATEOAS). I'll discuss some of these constraints shortly.

Layered System

REST was designed with the Internet in mind, which means that an architecture that follows REST is expected to work properly with the massive amount of traffic that exists in the web of webs.

To achieve this, the concept of *layers* is introduced (see Figure 1-5). By separating components into layers, and allowing each layer to only use the one below and to communicate its output to the one above, you simplify the system's overall complexity and keep component coupling in check. This is a great benefit in all type of systems, especially when the complexity of such a system is ever-growing (e.g., systems with massive amounts of clients, systems that are currently evolving, etc.).

The main disadvantage of this constraint is that for small systems, it might add unwanted latency into the overall data flow, due to the different interactions between layers.

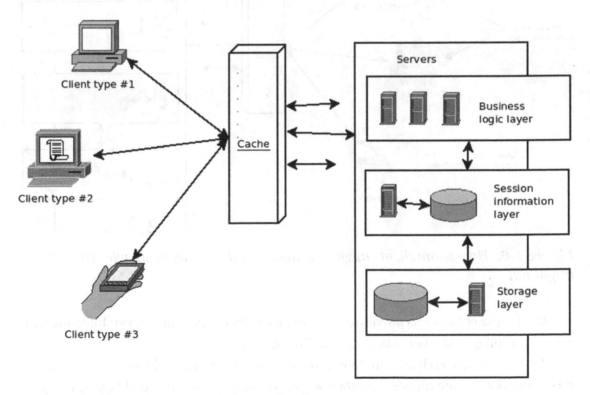

Figure 1-5. *Example of a multilayered architecture*

Code-on-Demand

Code-on-demand is the only optional constraint imposed by REST, which means that an architect using REST can choose whether or not to use this constraint and either gains its advantages or suffers its disadvantages.

With this constraint, the client can download and execute code provided by the server (such as Java applets, JavaScript scripts, etc.). In the case of REST APIs (on which this book focuses), this constraint seems unnecessary, because the normal thing for an API client to do is just get information from an endpoint, and then process it however needed; but for other uses of REST, like web servers, a client (i.e., a browser) will probably benefit from this constraint (see Figure 1-6).

Figure 1-6. *How some clients might execute the code-on-demand, whereas others might not*

All of these constraints provide a set of virtual walls within which an architecture can move and still gain the benefits of the REST design style.

But let's take a step back. I initially defined REST as a design style for representational state transfer; in other words, you transfer the state of things by using *some kind* of representation. But what are these "*things*"? The main focus of a REST architecture is the resources, the owners of the state that you're transferring. Just like in a real state (almost), it's all about resources, resources, resources.

Resources, Resources, Resources

The main building blocks of a REST architecture are the *resources*. Anything that can be named can be a resource (a web page, an image, a person, a weather service report, etc.). Resources define what the services are going to be about, the type of information that is going to be transferred, and their related actions. The resource is the main entity from which everything else is born.

A resource is the abstraction of anything that can be conceptualized (from an image file, to a plain text document). The structure of a resource is shown in Table 1-1.

Table 1-1. *Resource Structure Description*

Property	Description
Representations	It can be any way of representing data (binary, JSON, XML, etc.). A single resource can have multiple representations.
Identifier	A URL that retrieves only one specific resource *at any given time.*
Metadata	Content-type, last-modified time, and so forth.
Control data	Is-modified-since, cache-control.

Representations

At its core, a *representation* is a set of bytes, and some metadata that describes these bytes. A single resource can have more than one representation; just think of a weather service report (which could act as a possible resource).

The weather report for a single day could potentially return the following information:

- The date the report is referencing

- The maximum temperature for the day

- The minimum temperature for the day

- The temperature unit to be used

- A humidity percentage

- A code indicating how cloudy the day will be (e.g., high, medium, low)

11

Now that the resource's structure is defined, here are a few possible representations of the same resource:

```
JSON
{
    "date": "2014-10-25",
    "max_temp": 25.5,
    "min_temp": 10.0,
    "temp_unit": "C",
    "humidity_percentage": 75.0,
    "cloud_coverage": "low"
}
```

```
XML
<?xml version='1.0' encoding="UTF-8" ?>
<root>
    <temp_unit value="C" />
    <humidity_percentage value="75.0" />
    <cloud_coverage value="low" />
    <date value="2014-10-25" />
    <min_temp value="10.0" />
    <max_temp value="25.5" />
</root>
```

Custom pipe-separated values:

```
2014-10-25|25.5|10.0|C|75.0|low
```

And there could be many more. They all successfully represent the resource correctly; it is up to the client to read and parse the information. Even when the resource has more than one representation, it is common for clients (due to simplicity of development) to only request one of them. Unless you're doing some sort of consistency check against the API, there is no point in requesting more than one representation of the same resource, is there?

There are two very popular ways to let the client request a specific representation on a resource that has more than one. The first one directly follows the principles described by REST (when using HTTP as a basis), called *content negotiation*, which is part of the HTTP standard. The second one is a simplified version of this, with limited benefits. For the sake of completeness, I'll quickly go over them both.

Content Negotiation

As mentioned, this methodology is part of the HTTP standard,[5] so it's the preferred way according to REST (at least when focused on API development on top of HTTP). It is also more flexible and provides further advantages than the other method.

It consists of the client sending a specific header with the information of the different content types (or types of representations) supported, with an optional indicator of how supported/preferred that format is.

Let's look at an example from the "Content Negotiation" page on Wikipedia[6]:

```
Accept: text/html; q=1.0, text/*; q=0.8, image/gif; q=0.6, image/jpeg;
q=0.6, image/*; q=0.5, */*; q=0.1
```

This example is from a browser configured to accept various types of resources, but preferring HTML over plain text and GIF or JPEG images over other types, but ultimately accepts any other content type as a last resort.

On the server side, the API is in charge of reading this header and finding the best representation for each resource, based on the client's preferences.

Using File Extensions

Even though this approach is not part of the REST proposed style, it is widely used and a fairly simple alternative to the somewhat more complex other option, so I'll cover it anyway.

During the last few years, using file extensions has become an alternative preferred over using content negotiation; it is a simpler version and it doesn't rely on a header being sent; instead, it works with the concept of file extensions.

The extension portion of the file's name indicates the content type to the operating system and any other software trying to use it; so in the following case, the extension added to the resource's URL (unique identifier) indicates to the server the type of representation wanted.

```
GET /api/v1/books.json
GET /api/v1/books.xml
```

Both identifiers reference the same resource—the list of books, but they request a different representation of it.

---

[5]See http://tools.ietf.org/html/rfc7231#section-5.3.
[6]See https://en.wikipedia.org/wiki/Content_negotiation

> **Note** This approach might seem easier to implement, and even understand, by humans, but it lacks the flexibility added by content negotiation and should only be used if there is no real need for complex cases where multiple content types might be specified with their related preference.

Resource Identifier

The resource identifier should provide a unique way of identification at any given moment and it should provide the full path to the resource. A classic mistake is to assume it's the resource's ID on the storage medium used (i.e., the ID on the database). This means that you cannot consider a simple numeric ID as a resource identifier; you must provide the full path, and because we're basing REST on HTTP, the way to access the resource it to provide its full URI (*unique resource identifier*).

There is one more aspect to consider: the identifier of each resource must be able to reference it unequivocally at any given moment in time. This is an important distinction, because a URI like the following might reference *Harry Potter and the Half Blood Prince* for a certain period of time, and then *Harry Potter and the Deathly Hollows* 1 year later.:

```
GET /api/v1/books/last
```

This renders that URI as an invalid resource ID. Instead, each book needs a unique URI that is certain to not change over time; for example:

```
GET /api/v1/books/j-k-rowling/harry-potter-and-the-deathly-hollows
GET /api/v1/books/j-k-rowling/harry-potter-and-the-half-blood-prince
```

The identifiers are unique here, because you can safely assume that the author won't publish more books with the same title.

And to provide a valid example for getting the last book, you might consider doing something like this:

```
GET /api/v1/books?limit=1&sort=created_at
```

The preceding URI references the lists of books, and it asks for only one, sorted by its publication date, thus rendering the last book added.

Actions

Identifying a resource is easy: you know how to access it and you even know how to request for a specific format (if there is more than one); but that's not all that REST proposes. Since REST is using the HTTP protocol as a standing point, the latter provides a set of verbs that can be used to reference the type of action being done over a resource.

There are other actions, aside from accessing, that a client app can take in the resources provided by an API; these depend on the service provided by the API. These actions could potentially be anything, just like the type of resources handled by the system. Still, there is a set of common actions that any system that is resource-oriented should be able to provide: CRUD (create, retrieve, update, and delete) actions.

These so-called actions can be directly mapped to the HTTP verbs, but REST does not enforce a standardized way to do so. However, there are some actions that are naturally derived by the verb and others that have been standardized by the API development community over the years, as shown in Table 1-2.

Table 1-2. *HTTP Verbs and Their Proposed Actions*

HTTP Verb	Proposed Action
GET	Access a resource in a read-only mode
POST	Normally used to send a new resource into the server (create action)
PUT	Normally used to update a given resource (update action)
DELETE	Used to delete a resource
HEAD	Not part of the CRUD actions, but the verb is used to ask if a given resource exists without returning any of its representations
OPTIONS	Not part of the CRUD actions, but used to retrieve a list of available verbs on a given resource (i.e., What can the client do with a specific resource?)

That said, a client may or may not support all of these actions; it depends on what needs to be achieved. For instance, web browsers—a clear and common example of a REST client—only have support for GET and POST verbs from within the HTML code of a page, such as links and forms (although using the XMLHttpRequest object from JavaScript would provide support for the major verbs mentioned earlier).

15

> **Note**   The list of verbs and their corresponding actions are *suggestions*. For instance, there are some developers who prefer to switch PUT and POST, by having PUT add new elements and POST update them.

Complex Actions

CRUD actions are normally required, but they're just a very small subset of the entire spectrum of actions that a client can do with a specific resource or set of resources.

For instance, take common actions like searching, filtering, working with subresources (e.g., the books of an author, the reviews of a book, etc.), sharing a blogpost, and so forth. All of these actions fail to directly match one of the verbs that I mentioned.

The first solution that many developers succumb to is to specify the action taken as part of the URL; so you might end up with things like the following:

```
GET /api/v1/blogpost/12342/like
```

```
GET /api/v1/books/search
```

```
GET /api/v1/authors/filtering
```

Those URLs break the URI principle, because they're not referencing a unique resource at any given time; instead, they're referencing an action on a resource (or group of resources). They might seem like a good idea at first, but in the long run, and if the system keeps on growing, there will be too many URLs, which will increase the complexity of the client using the API.

So to keep things simple, use the following rule of thumb: *Hide the complexity of your actions behind the "?".*

This rule can apply to all verbs, not just GET, and can help achieve complex actions without compromising the URL complexity of the API. For the preceding examples, the URIs could become something like this:

```
PUT /api/v1/blogposts/12342?action=like
```

```
GET /api/v1/books?q=[SEARCH-TERM]
```

```
GET /api/v1/authors?filters=[COMMA SEPARATED LIST OF FILTERS]
```

Notice how the first one changed from a GET to a PUT due to the fact that the action is updating a resource by linking it.

But what happens when the "?" is not enough?

When the complexity of your actions is too much for the "?", there are some alternatives that walk the line when it comes to REST-compliant solutions. Some of them might not be ideal or even desired for your API design, but when reality hits you need to do the best you can and that also includes figuring out if your use case actually fits inside REST or if you need to go another route.

Use Collection of Actions

An alternative way of dealing with complex actions inside your API is to treat them as resource collections. Granted, this is a bit of a stretch to what an action actually is, but like I said, we're walking the line here guys.

What this provides, is a valid interface for you to send commands to your resources following a REST-like approach.

For example, say you want to reboot a VM, you can do something like the following:

```
POST /virtual-machines/<your-vm-id>/reboots
{
 "When": "now"
}
```

This would effectively send a reboot command to your VM, telling it to reboot right now. Notice the use of the POST verb here; there are couple reasons why I used that one and not others:

1. Since we're treating actions as resources, executing a new action is the equivalent of creating a new resource inside the action's collection

2. POST is not an idempotent operation, which fits this use case, since we can't be certain about the side effects your complex actions could have.

You could even extend this concept a bit further and provide an actual functionality to other verbs on this endpoint, such as GET, so something like this:

```
GET /virtual-machines/<your-vm-id>/reboots
```

would provide an output detailing the list of reboots created or, put another way, a list of times the action was executed:

```
{
    "reboots": [
        { "received": "2001-10-23 13:30:00+0100", "params": { "when": "now" } },
        { "received": "2001-12-03 03:30:00+0100", "params": { "when": "5 min" } },
        { "received": "2002-10-23 13:30:00+0100", "params": { "when": "now" } }
    ]
}
```

Furthermore, each action could provide an endpoint to return information about it, such as documentation to help developers using them. For instance, a request such as:

```
GET /virtual-machines/<your-vm-id>/reboots/1
```

could return something like:

```
{
    "last-executed": "2018-02-23 15:02:02+0300",
    "params": {
        "when":  {
            "Required": true,
            "Docs": "Describes the system reboot needs to take place,
            relative to the moment the action is processed"
        }
    }
}
```

Another classic problematic endpoint that REST APIs tend to have is the so-called "search endpoint," one that can't always fit inside our resource-based schema.

And for this, we have a couple of options.

Single-Entity Searches

If the search functionality is only going to return, and overall deal with, one kind of entity, or if you're going to provide scoped searches (meaning you will always be searching on specific collections), then you can probably hide the search feature behind the listing endpoint and use GET requests with search parameters

```
GET /books/?q=Harry pott&p=1&size=10
```

The previous example simply hijacks the listing endpoint and adds the ability to filter the results but accepting a search string. These parameters could even be optional, rendering this endpoint quite powerful and versatile.

Note The endpoint you define for your search functionality does not ensure the type of results you'll get, that will depend on the underlying technology used. If you're looking for simple searches, a quick SQL query can give you the results you're looking for. But if you need something more complex, I would suggest looking into solutions such as Elastic.

Multi-Entity Searches

Now, if instead of just looking for books, you actually want your user to look for books and also for author's bios, and client names. All at the same time and have those results all mixed in as one single list. Then there is no real easy way to relate this type of search to a single resource, is there?

In this case, the only option that we have is to bite the bullet and break the mantra; in other words, create an endpoint that references the actual action instead of a single resource, i.e:

```
GET /search?q=Harry&p=1&size=10
```

If you can, and as long as it makes sense, always try to use endpoints such as GET/action to provide information about the action and POST /action to perform it.

In the end, if you end up having to "bite the bullet" a lot while designing the endpoints of your system, then maybe REST is not the best paradigm for you.

Hypermedia in the Response and Main Entry Point

To make REST's interface uniform, several constraints must be applied. One of them is *Hypermedia as the Engine of Application State*, also known as *HATEOAS*. I'll go over what that concept means, how it is meant to be applied by a RESTful system, and finally, how you end up with a great new feature that allows any RESTful system client to start the interaction knowing only a single endpoint of the entire system (the root endpoint).

Again, the structure of a resource contains a section called *metadata*; inside that section, the representation of every resource should contain a set of hypermedia links that let the client know what to do with each resource. By providing this information in the response itself, the next steps any client can take are there, thus providing an even greater level of decoupling between client and server.

Changes to the resource identifiers, or added and removed functionalities, can be provided through this method without affecting the client at all, or at worst, with minimal impact.

Think of a web browser: all it needs to help a user navigate through a favorite site is the home page URL; after that, the following actions are presented inside the representation (HTML code) as links. Those are the only logical next steps that the user can take, and from there, new links will be presented, and so on.

In the case of a RESTful service, the same thing can be said: by calling upon the main endpoint (also known as *bookmark* or *root endpoint*), the client will discover all possible first steps (normally things like resource lists and other relevant endpoints).

Let's look at an example in Listing 1-1.

Root endpoint: GET /api/v1/

Listing 1-1. Example of a JSON Response from the Root Endpoint

```
{
    "metadata": {
        "links": {
            "books": {
                "uri": "/books",
                "content-type": "application/json"
            },
            "authors": {
                "uri": "/authors",
```

```
            "content-type": "application/json"
        }
      }
    }
}
```

Now let's look at the books list endpoint's results in Listing 1-2: GET `/api/v1/books`

Listing 1-2. Example of Another JSON Response with Hyperlinks to Other Resources

```
{
 "resources": [
  {
   "title": "Harry Potter and the Half Blood prince",
   "description": "......",
   "author": {
    "name": "J.K.Rowling",
    "metadata": {
     "links": {
      "data": {
       "uri": "/authors/j-k-rowling",
       "content-type": "application/json"
      },
      "books": {
       "uri": "/authors/j-k-rowling/books",
       "content-type": "application/json"
      }
     }
    }
   },
   "copies": 10
  },
  {
   "title": "Dune",
   "description": "......",
   "author": {
```

```
      "name": "Frank Herbert",
      "metadata": {
        "links": {
          "data": {
            "uri": "/authors/frank-herbert",
            "content-type": "application/json"
          },
          "books": {
            "uri": "/authors/frank-herbert/books",
            "content-type": "application/json"
          }
        }
      },
      "copies": 5
    }
  ],
  "total": 100,
  "metadata": {
    "links": {
      "next": {
        "uri": "/books?page=1",
        "content-type": "application/json"
      }
    }
  }
}
```

There are three sections highlighted in preceding example (Listing 1-2); those are the links returned on the response. With that information, the client application knows the following logical steps:

1. How to get the information from the books authors

2. How to get the list of books by the authors

3. How to get the next page of results

Note that the full list of authors is not accessible through this endpoint; this is because for this particular use case, it's not needed, so the API just doesn't return it. It was present on the root endpoint, though, so if the client needs it when displaying the information to the end-user, it should still have it available.

Each link from the preceding example contains an attribute specifying the content-type of the representation of that resource. If the resources have more than one possible representation, the different formats could be added as different links inside each resource's metadata element, letting the client choose the most adequate to the current use case, or the type could change based on the client's preferences (content negotiation).

Note that the earlier JSON structure (more specifically, the metadata elements' structure) is not important. The relevant part of the example is the information presented in the response. Each server has the freedom to design the structure as needed.

Not having a standard structure might harm the developer experience while interacting with your system, so it might be a good idea to adopt one. This is certainly not enforced by REST, but it would be a major point in favor of your system. A good standard to adopt in this case would be *Hypertext Application Language*, or HAL,[7] which tries to create a standard for both XML and JSON when representing resources with those languages.

A Few Notes on HAL

HAL tries to define a representation as having two major elements: resources and links.

According to HAL, a resource has links, embedded resources (other resources associated to their parent), and a state (the actual properties that describe the resource). On the other hand, links have a target (the URI), a relation, and some other optional properties to deal with deprecation, content negotiation, and so forth.

---

[7]See http://stateless.co/hal_specification.html.

Listing 1-3 shows the preceding example represented using the HAL format.

Listing 1-3. JSON Response Following the HAL Standard

```json
{
  "_embedded": [
    {
      "title": "Harry Potter and the Half Blood prince",
      "description": "......",
      "copies": 10,
      "_embedded": {
        "author": {
          "name": "J.K.Rowling",
          "_links": {
            "self": {
              "href": "/authors/j-k-rowling",
              "type": "application/json+hal"
            },
            "books": {
              "href": "/authors/j-k-rowling/books",
              "type": "application/json+hal"
            }
          }
        }
      }
    },
    {
      "title": "Dune",
      "description": "......",
      "copies": 5,
      "_embedded": {
        "author": {
          "name": "Frank Herbert",
```

```
      "_links": {
        "self": {
          "href": "/authors/frank-herbert",
          "type": "application/json+hal"
        },
        "books": {
          "href": "/authors/frank-herbert/books",
          "type": "application/json+hal"
        }
      }
    }
  }
],
"total": 100,
"_links": {
  "self": {
    "href": "/books",
    "type": "application/json+hal"
  },
  "next": {
    "href": "/books?page=1",
    "type": "application/json+hal"
  }
}
}
```

The main change in Listing 1-3 is that the actual books have been moved inside an element called "_embedded", as the standard dictates, since they're actual embedded documents inside the represented resource, which is the list of books (the only property that belongs to the resource is "total", representing the total number of results). The same can be said for the authors, now inside the "_embedded" element of each book.

Status Codes

Another interesting standard that REST can benefit from when based on HTTP is the usage of HTTP status codes.[8]

A *status code* is a number that summarizes the response associated to it. There are some common ones, like 404 for "Page not found," or 200 for "OK," or the always helpful 500 for "Internal server error" (that was irony, in case it wasn't clear enough).

A status code is helpful for clients to begin interpreting the response, but in most cases, it shouldn't be a substitute for it. As the API owner, you can't really transmit in the response what exactly caused a crash on your side by just replying with the number 500. There are some cases, though, when a number is enough, like 404; although a good response will always return information that should help the client solve the problem (with a 404, a link to the home page or the root URL are good places to start).

These codes are grouped in five sets, based on their meaning:

- *1xx*: Informational and only defined under HTTP 1.1.

- *2xx*: The request went OK, here's your content.

- *3xx*: The resource was moved somehow to somewhere.

- *4xx*: The source of the request did something wrong.

- *5xx*: The server crashed due to some error in its code.

With that in mind, Table 1-3 lists some classic status codes that an API could potentially use.

---

[8]See http://www.w3.org/Protocols/rfc2616/rfc2616-sec10.html.

Table 1-3. *HTTP Status Codes and Their Related Interpretation*

Status Code	Meaning
200	*OK.* The request went fine and the content requested was returned. This is normally used on GET requests.
201	*Created.* The resource was created and the server has acknowledged it. It could be useful on responses to POST or PUT requests. Additionally, the new resource could be returned as part of the response body.
204	*No content.* The action was successful but there is no content returned. Useful for actions that do not require a response body, such as a DELETE action.
301	*Moved permanently.* This resource was moved to another location and the location is returned. This header is especially useful when URLs change over time (maybe due to a change in version, a migration, or some other disruptive change), keeping the old ones and returning a redirection to the new location allows old clients to update their references in their own time.
400	*Bad request.* The request issued has problems (for example, might be lacking some required parameters). A good addition to a 400 response might be an error message that a developer can use to fix the request.
401	*Unauthorized.* Especially useful for authentication when the requested resource is not accessible to the user owning the request.
403	*Forbidden.* The resource is not accessible, but unlike 401, authentication will not affect the response.
404	*Not found.* The URL provided does not identify any resource. A good addition to this response could be a set of valid URLs that the client can use to get back on track (root URL, previous URL used, etc.).
405	*Method not allowed.* The HTTP verb used on a resource is not allowed—for instance, doing a PUT on a resource that is read-only.
500	*Internal server error.* A generic error code when an unexpected condition is met and the server crashes. Normally, this response is accompanied by an error message explaining what went wrong.

Note   To see the full list of HTTP status codes and their meanings, please refer to the RFC of HTTP 1.1.[9]

REST vs. the Past

Before REST was all cool and hip, and every business out there wanted to provide their clients with a RESTful API in their service, there were other options for developers who wanted to interconnect systems. These are still being used on old services or by services that required their specific features, but less and less so every year.

Back in the 1990s, the software industry started to think about system interoperability and how two (or more) computers could achieve it. Some solutions were born, such as COM,[10] created by Microsoft, and CORBA,[11] created by the Object Management Group. These were the first two implementations back then, but they had a major issue: they were not compatible with each other.

Other solutions arose, like RMI (Remote Method Invocation), but it was meant specifically for Java, which meant it was technology-dependent, and hadn't really caught up with the development community.

By 1997, Microsoft decided to research solutions that would use XML as the main transport language and would allow systems to interconnect using RPC (Remote Procedure Call) over HTTP, thus achieving a somewhat technology-independent solution that would considerably simplify system interconnectivity. That research gave birth to XML-RPC around 1998.

Listing 1-4 is a classic XML-RPC request taken from Wikipedia:[12]

---

[9]See http://tools.ietf.org/html/rfc7231#section-6.

[10]See https://en.wikipedia.org/wiki/Component_Object_Model

[11]See http://www.corba.org/.

[12]See http://en.wikipedia.org/wiki/XML-RPC.

Listing 1-4. Example of an XML-RPC Request

```xml
<?xml version="1.0"?>
<methodCall>
  <methodName>examples.getStateName</methodName>
  <params>
    <param>
        <value><i4>40</i4></value>
    </param>
  </params>
</methodCall>
```

Listing 1-5 shows a possible response.

Listing 1-5. Example of an XML-RPC Response

```xml
<?xml version="1.0"?>
<methodResponse>
  <params>
    <param>
        <value><string>South Dakota</string></value>
    </param>
  </params>
</methodResponse>
```

From the examples shown in Listing 1-4 and Listing 1-5, it is quite clear that the messages (both requests and responses) were overly verbose, something that was directly related to the use of XML. There are implementations of XML-RPC that exist today for several operating systems and programming languages, like Apache XML-RPC[13] (written in Java), XMLRPC-EPI[14] (written in C), and XML-RPC-C[15] for C and C++ (see Figure 1-7).

---

[13]See http://ws.apache.org/xmlrpc/.

[14]See http://xmlrpc-epi.sourceforge.net.

[15]See http://xmlrpc-c.sourceforge.net/.

Figure 1-7. *Diagram showing the basic architecture of an XML-RPC interaction*

After XML-RPC became more popular, it mutated into SOAP,[16] a more standardized and formalized version of the same principle. SOAP still uses XML as the transport language, but the message format is now richer (and therefore complex). Listing 1-6 is an example from W3C's specification page on SOAP:

Listing 1-6. Example of a SOAP Request

```
<?xml version='1.0' ?>
<env:Envelope xmlns:env="http://www.w3.org/2003/05/soap-envelope">
 <env:Header>
  <m:reservation xmlns:m="http://travelcompany.example.org/reservation"
          env:role="http://www.w3.org/2003/05/soap-envelope/role/next"
           env:mustUnderstand="true">
   <m:reference>uuid:093a2da1-q345-739r-ba5d-pqff98fe8j7d</m:reference>
   <m:dateAndTime>2001-11-29T13:20:00.000-05:00</m:dateAndTime>
  </m:reservation>
```

---

[16]See http://www.w3.org/TR/soap/.

```
  <n:passenger xmlns:n="http://mycompany.example.com/employees"
          env:role="http://www.w3.org/2003/05/soap-envelope/role/next"
          env:mustUnderstand="true">
    <n:name>Åke Jógvan Øyvind</n:name>
  </n:passenger>
</env:Header>
<env:Body>
 <p:itinerary
   xmlns:p="http://travelcompany.example.org/reservation/travel">
  <p:departure>
    <p:departing>New York</p:departing>
    <p:arriving>Los Angeles</p:arriving>
    <p:departureDate>2001-12-14</p:departureDate>
    <p:departureTime>late afternoon</p:departureTime>
    <p:seatPreference>aisle</p:seatPreference>
  </p:departure>
  <p:return>
    <p:departing>Los Angeles</p:departing>
    <p:arriving>New York</p:arriving>
    <p:departureDate>2001-12-20</p:departureDate>
    <p:departureTime>mid-morning</p:departureTime>
    <p:seatPreference/>
  </p:return>
 </p:itinerary>
 <q:lodging
   xmlns:q="http://travelcompany.example.org/reservation/hotels">
  <q:preference>none</q:preference>
 </q:lodging>
</env:Body>
</env:Envelope>
```

Figure 1-8 shows the basic structure of the example from Listing 1-6.

Figure 1-8. *Image from the W3C SOAP spec page*

SOAP services are actually dependent on another technology called Web Service Description Language (WSDL). An XML-based language, it describes the services provided to clients that want to consume them.

Listing 1-7 is an annotated WSDL example taken from the W3C web site.[17]

Listing 1-7. WSDL Example

```
<?xml version="1.0"?>

<!-- root element wsdl:definitions defines set of related services -->
<wsdl:definitions name="EndorsementSearch"
  targetNamespace="http://namespaces.snowboard-info.com"
  xmlns:es="http://www.snowboard-info.com/EndorsementSearch.wsdl"
  xmlns:esxsd="http://schemas.snowboard-info.com/EndorsementSearch.xsd"
```

---

[17]See http://www.w3.org/2001/03/14-annotated-WSDL-examples.

```
xmlns:soap="http://schemas.xmlsoap.org/wsdl/soap/"
xmlns:wsdl="http://schemas.xmlsoap.org/wsdl/">

<!-- wsdl:types encapsulates schema definitions of communication types;
here using xsd -->
<wsdl:types>

  <!-- all type declarations are in a chunk of xsd -->
  <xsd:schema targetNamespace="http://namespaces.snowboard-info.com"
     xmlns:xsd="http://www.w3.org/1999/XMLSchema">

    <!-- xsd definition: GetEndorsingBoarder [manufacturer string, model
    string] -->
    <xsd:element name="GetEndorsingBoarder">
    <xsd:complexType>
      <xsd:sequence>
        <xsd:element name="manufacturer" type="string"/>
        <xsd:element name="model" type="string"/>
      </xsd:sequence>
     </xsd:complexType>
    </xsd:element>

    <!-- xsd definition: GetEndorsingBoarderResponse [... endorsingBoarder
    string ...] -->
    <xsd:element name="GetEndorsingBoarderResponse">
    <xsd:complexType>
      <xsd:all>
        <xsd:element name="endorsingBoarder" type="string"/>
      </xsd:all>
    </xsd:complexType>
    </xsd:element>

    <!-- xsd definition: GetEndorsingBoarderFault [... errorMessage
    string ...] -->
    <xsd:element name="GetEndorsingBoarderFault">
    <xsd:complexType>
      <xsd:all>
        <xsd:element name="errorMessage" type="string"/>
```

```
        </xsd:all>
      </xsd:complexType>
      </xsd:element>

    </xsd:schema>
</wsdl:types>

<!-- wsdl:message elements describe potential transactions -->

<!-- request GetEndorsingBoarderRequest is of type GetEndorsingBoarder -->
<wsdl:message name="GetEndorsingBoarderRequest">
  <wsdl:part name="body" element="esxsd:GetEndorsingBoarder"/>
</wsdl:message>

<!-- response GetEndorsingBoarderResponse is of type GetEndorsingBoarder
Response -->
<wsdl:message name="GetEndorsingBoarderResponse">
  <wsdl:part name="body" element="esxsd:GetEndorsingBoarderResponse"/>
</wsdl:message>

<!-- wsdl:portType describes messages in an operation -->
<wsdl:portType name="GetEndorsingBoarderPortType">

  <!-- the value of wsdl:operation eludes me -->
  <wsdl:operation name="GetEndorsingBoarder">
    <wsdl:input message="es:GetEndorsingBoarderRequest"/>
    <wsdl:output message="es:GetEndorsingBoarderResponse"/>
    <wsdl:fault message="es:GetEndorsingBoarderFault"/>
  </wsdl:operation>
</wsdl:portType>

<!-- wsdl:binding states a serialization protocol for this service -->
<wsdl:binding name="EndorsementSearchSoapBinding"
            type="es:GetEndorsingBoarderPortType">

  <!-- leverage off soap:binding document style @@@(no wsdl:foo pointing
  at the soap binding) -->
  <soap:binding style="document"
              transport="http://schemas.xmlsoap.org/soap/http"/>
```

```xml
<!-- semi-opaque container of network transport details classed by
soap:binding above @@@ -->
<wsdl:operation name="GetEndorsingBoarder">

    <!-- again bind to SOAP? @@@ -->
    <soap:operation soapAction="http://www.snowboard-info.com/
    EndorsementSearch"/>

    <!-- furthur specify that the messages in the wsdl:operation
    "GetEndorsingBoarder" use SOAP? @@@ -->
    <wsdl:input>
       <soap:body use="literal"
                namespace="http://schemas.snowboard-info.com/
                EndorsementSearch.xsd"/>
    </wsdl:input>
    <wsdl:output>
       <soap:body use="literal"
                namespace="http://schemas.snowboard-info.com/
                EndorsementSearch.xsd"/>
    </wsdl:output>
    <wsdl:fault>
       <soap:body use="literal"
                namespace="http://schemas.snowboard-info.com/
                EndorsementSearch.xsd"/>
    </wsdl:fault>
  </wsdl:operation>
</wsdl:binding>

<!-- wsdl:service names a new service "EndorsementSearchService" -->
<wsdl:service name="EndorsementSearchService">
  <wsdl:documentation>snowboarding-info.com Endorsement Service</wsdl:
  documentation>

  <!-- connect it to the binding "EndorsementSearchSoapBinding" above -->
  <wsdl:port name="GetEndorsingBoarderPort"
            binding="es:EndorsementSearchSoapBinding">
```

```
<!-- give the binding an network address -->
<soap:address location="http://www.snowboard-info.com/
EndorsementSearch"/>
    </wsdl:port>
  </wsdl:service>

</wsdl:definitions>
```

The main drawback of these types of services was the amount of information used, both to describe them and to use them. Even though XML provided the much-required technology agnostic means of encoding data to be transmitted between two systems, it also blotted the message sent quite noticeably.

Both of these technologies (XML-RPC and SOAP + WSDL) provided the solution to system interconnectivity at a time when it was required. They provided a way to transmit messages using a "universal" language between all systems, but they also had several major issues compared to today's leading standard (see Table 1-4). This can be clearly seen, for example, in the way developers feel about using XML instead of JSON.

Table 1-4. *Comparison of XML-RPC/SOAP and REST Services*

XML-RCP/SOAP	REST
Specific SOAP clients had to be created for each programming language. Even though XML was universal, a new client would have to be coded to parse the WSDL to understand how the service worked.	REST is completely technology-agnostic and doesn't require special clients, only a programming language capable of connectivity through the chosen protocol (e.g., HTTP, FTP, etc.).
The client needs to know everything about the service before initiating the interaction (thus the WSDL mentioned earlier).	The client only needs to know the main root endpoint, and with the hypermedia provided on the response, self-discovery is possible.
Because the service was used from within the client source code and called a specific function or method from within the server's code, the coupling between those two systems was too big. A rewrite of the server code would probably lead to a rewrite on the client's code.	The interface is implementation-independent; the complete server-side code can be rewritten and the API's interface will not have to be changed.

Note   Comparing XML-RPC/SOAP with REST might not be entirely fair (or possible) due to the fact that the first two are protocols, whereas the latter is an architectural style; but some points can still be compared if you keep that distinction in mind.

Summary

This chapter was a small overview of what REST is meant to be and the kind of benefits a system will gain by following the REST style. The chapter also covered a few extra principles, like HTTP verbs and status codes, which despite not being part of the REST style, are indeed part of the HTTP standard, the protocol we're basing this book on.

Finally, I discussed the main technologies used prior to REST, and you saw how they compared to the current leading industry standard.

In the next chapter, I'll go over some good API design practices, and you'll see how you can achieve them using REST.

CHAPTER 2

API Design Best Practices

The practice of API design is a tricky one. Even when there are so many options out there—tools to use, standards to apply, styles to follow—there is one basic question that needs to be answered and needs to be clear in the developer's mind before any kind design and development can begin...

What Defines a Good API?

As we all know, the concepts of "good" and "bad" are very subjective (one could probably read a couple of books discussing this on its own), and therefore, opinions vary from one person to another. That being said, years of experience of dealing with different kinds of APIs have left the developer community (and this author) with a pretty good sense of the need-to-have features of any good API. (Disclaimer: Things like clean code, good development practices, and other internal considerations will not be mentioned here but will be assumed, since they should be part of every software undertaking.)

So let's go over this list.

- *Developer-friendly*: The developers working with your API should not suffer when dealing with your system.

- *Extensibility*: Your system should be able to handle the addition of new features without breaking your clients.

- *Up-to-date documentation*: Good documentation is key to your API being picked up by new developers.

- *Proper error handling*: Because things will go wrong and you need to be prepared.

- *Provides multiple SDK/libraries*: The more work you simplify for developers, the more they'll like your system.

© Fernando Doglio 2018
F. Doglio, *REST API Development with Node.js*, https://doi.org/10.1007/978-1-4842-3715-1_2

- *Security*: A key aspect of any global system.

- *Scalability*: The ability to scale up and down is something any good API should have to properly provide its services.

I'll go over these points one by one and show how they affect the API and how following the REST style help.

Developer-Friendly

By definition, an API is an *application programming interface*, with the key word being *interface*. When thinking about designing an API that will be used by developers other than yourself, there is a key aspect that needs to be taken into consideration: the Developer eXperience (or DX).

Even when the API will be used by another system, the integration into that system is first done by one or more developers—human beings that bring the human factor into that integration. This means you'll want the API to be as easy to use as possible, which makes for a great DX, and which should translate into more developers and client applications using the API.

There is a trade-off, though, since simplifying things for humans could lead into an oversimplification of the interface, which in turn could lead to design issues when dealing with complex functionalities.

It is important to consider the DX as one of the major aspects of an API (let's be honest, without developers using it, there is no point to an API), but there are other aspects that have to be considered and given weight in the design decisions. *Make it simple, but not dummy simple.*

The next sections provide some pointers for a good DX.

Communication's Protocol

This is one of the most basic aspects of the interface. When choosing a communication protocol, it's always a good idea to go with one that is familiar to the developers using the API. There are several standards that already have libraries and modules available in many programming languages (e.g., HTTP, FTP, SSH, etc.).

A custom-made protocol isn't always a good idea because you'll lose that instant portability in so many existing technologies. That said, if you're ready to create support libraries for the most used languages, and your custom protocol is more efficient for your use case, it could be the right choice.

In the end, it's up to the API designer to evaluate the best solution based on the context in which he's working.

In this book, you're working under the assumption that the protocol chosen for REST is HTTP.[1] It's a very well-known protocol; any modern programming language supports it and it's the basis for the entire Internet. You can rest assured that most developers have a basic understanding of how to use it. And if not, there is plenty of information out there to get to know it better.

In summary, there is no silver bullet protocol out there perfect for every scenario. Think about your API needs, make sure that whatever you choose is compatible with REST, and you'll be fine.

Easy-to-Remember Access Points

The points of contact between all client apps and the API are called *endpoints*. The API needs to provide them to allow clients to access its functionalities. This can be done through whatever communications protocol is chosen. These access points should have mnemotechnic names to help the developer understand their purpose just by reading them.

Of course, the name by itself should never be a replacement for a detailed documentation, but it is normally considered a good idea to reference the resource being used and to have some kind of indicator of the action being taken when calling that access point.

The following is a good example of a badly named access point (meant to list the books in a bookstore):

```
GET /books/action1
```

This example uses the HTTP protocol to specify the access point, and even though the entity used (books) is being referenced, the action name is not clear; action1 could mean anything, or even worse, the meaning could change in the future, but the name would still be suitable, so any existing client would undoubtedly break.

A better example—one that follows REST and the standards discussed in Chapter 1—would be this:

```
GET /books
```

---

[1]See http://www.w3.org/Protocols/rfc2616/rfc2616.html.

41

This should present the developer with more than enough information to understand that a GET request into the root of a resource (/books) will always yield a list of items of this type; then the developer can replicate this pattern into other resources, as long as the interface is kept uniform across all other endpoints.

Uniform Interface

Easy-to-remember access points are important, but so is being consistent when defining them. Again, you have to go back to the human factor when consuming an API: you're a human too. So making the lives of the developers using your APIs easier is a must if you want anyone to use it, you can't forget about the DX. That means you need to be consistent when defining endpoints' names, request formats, and response formats. There can be more than one version for the latter two (more specifically, the response format is directly tied to the various representations a resource can have), but as long as the default is always the same, there will be no problems.

A good example of an inconsistent interface, even though not on an API, can be seen in the programming language PHP. It has underscore notation on most functions' names, but the underscore is not used on some, so the developer is always forced to go back to the documentation to check how to write these functions (or worse, rely on his/her memory).

For example, `str_replace` is a function that uses an underscore to separate both words (`str` and `replace`), whereas `htmlentities` has no separation of words at all.

Another example of bad design practice in an API is to name the endpoints based on the actions taken instead of the resources handled; for example:

```
/getAllBooks
/submitNewBook
/updateAuthor
/getBooksAuthors
/getNumberOfBooksOnStock
```

These examples clearly show the pattern that this API is following. And at first glance, they might not seem that bad, but consider how poor the interface is going to become as new features and resources are added to the system (not to mention if the actions are modified). Each new addition to the system causes extra endpoints to the API's interface. The developers of client apps will have no clue as to how these new endpoints are named. For instance, if the API is extended to support the cover images of books, with the current naming scheme, these are all possible new endpoints:

```
/addNewImageToBook
/getBooksImages
/addCoverImage
/listBooksCovers
```

And the list can go on. So for any real-world application, you can safely assume that following this type of pattern will yield a really big list of endpoints, increasing the complexity of both server-side code and client-side code. It will also hurt the system's ability to capture new developers, due to the inherited complexity that it will have over the years.

To solve this problem and generate an easy-to-use and uniform interface across the entire API, you can apply the REST style to the endpoints. If you remember the constraints proposed by REST from Chapter 1, you end up with a resource-centric interface. And thanks to HTTP, you also have verbs to indicate actions.

Table 2-1 shows how the previous interface changes using REST.

Table 2-1. *List of Endpoints and How They Change When the REST Style Is Applied*

Old Style	REST Style
/getAllBooks	GET /books
/submitNewBook	POST /books
/updateAuthor	PUT /authors/:id
/getBooksAuthors	GET /books/:id/authors
/getNumberOfBooksOnStock	GET /books (This number can easily be returned as part of this endpoint.)
/addNewImageToBook	PUT /books/:id
/getBooksImages	GET /books/:id/images
/addCoverImage	POST /books/:id/cover_image
/listBooksCovers	GET /books (This information can be returned in this endpoint using subresources.)

You went from having to remember nine different endpoints to just two, with the added bonus of having all HTTP verbs being the same in all cases once you defined the standard; now there is no need to remember specific roles in each case (they'll always mean the same thing).

Transport Language

Another aspect of the interface to consider is the *transport language* used. For many years, the de facto standard was XML; it provided a technology-agnostic way of expressing data that could easily be sent between clients and servers. Nowadays, there is a new standard gaining popularity over XML—JSON.

Why JSON?

JSON has been gaining traction over the past few years (see Figure 2-1) as the standard Data Transfer Format. This is mainly due to the advantages that it provides. The following lists just a few:

- It's lightweight. There are very little data in a JSON file that are not directly related to the information being transferred. This is a major winning point over more verbose formats like XML.[2]

- It's human-readable. The format itself is so simple that it can easily be read and written by a human. This is particularly important considering that a focus point of the interface of any good API is the human factor (otherwise known as the DX).

- It supports different data types. Because not everything being transferred is a string, this feature allows the developer to provide extra meaning to the information transferred.

---

[2]XML is not strictly a Data Transfer Format, but it's being used as one.

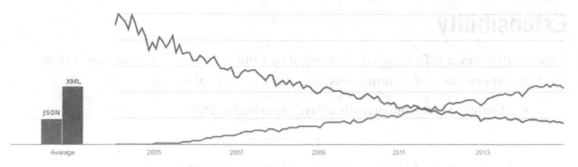

Figure 2-1. *Trend of Google searches for "JSON" vs. "XML" over the last few years*

The list could go on, but these are the three main aspects that are helping JSON win so many followers in the developer community.

Even though JSON is a great format and is gaining traction, it's not the silver bullet that will always solve all of your problems, so it's also important to provide clients with options. And here is where REST comes to help.

Since the protocol you're basing REST on is HTTP, developers can use a mechanism called *content negotiation* to allow clients to specify which of the supported formats they want to receive (as discussed in Chapter 1). This allows for more flexibility on the API and still keeps the interface uniform.

Going back to the list of endpoints, the last one talks about using a subresource as the solution. That can be interpreted in several ways, because not only is the language used to transfer the data important, but so is the structure that you give the data being transferred. My final advice for a uniform interface is to standardize the format used, or even better, follow an existing one, like *Hypertext Application Language* (HAL).

This was covered in Chapter 1, so refer back to it for more information.

Extensibility

A good API is never fully finished. This might be a bold claim, but it's one that comes from the experience of the community. Let's look at some of the big ones.[3]

- Google APIs: 5 billion calls a day;[4] launched in 2005

- Facebook APIs: 5 billion calls a day;[5] launched in 2007

- Twitter APIs: 13 billion calls a day;[6] launched in 2006

These examples show that even when a great team is behind the API, the APIs will keep growing and changing because the client apps developers find new ways to use it, the business model of the API owner changes over time, or simply because features are added and removed.

When any of this happens, the API may need to be extended or changed, and new access points added or old ones changed. If the original design is right, then going from v1 to v2 should be no problem, but if it's not, then that migration could spell disaster for everyone.

How Is Extensibility Managed?

When extending the API, you're basically releasing a new version of your software, so the first thing you need to do is let your users (the developers) know what will happen once the new version is out. Will their apps still work? Are the changes backward-compatible? Will you maintain several versions of your API online or just the latest one?

A good API should take the following points into consideration:

- How easily can new endpoints be added?

- Is the new version backward-compatible?

- Can clients continue to work with older versions of the API while their code is being updated?

- What will happen to existing clients targeting the new API?

---

[3]Source: http://www.slideshare.net/3scale/apis-for-biz-dev-20-which-business-model-15473323.

[4]Source: http://www.slideshare.net/3scale/apis-for-biz-dev-20-which-business-model-15473323, April 2010.

[5]Source: http://www.slideshare.net/3scale/apis-for-biz-dev-20-which-business-model-15473323, October 2009.

[6]Source: http://www.slideshare.net/3scale/apis-for-biz-dev-20-which-business-model-15473323, May 2011.

- How easy will it be for clients to target the new version of the API?

Once all these points are settled, then you can safely grow and extend the API.

Normally, going from version A to version B of an API by instantly deprecating version A and taking it offline in favor of version B is considered a bad move, unless, of course, you have very few client applications using that version.

A better approach for this type of situation is to allow developers to choose which version of the API they want to use, keeping the old version long enough to let everyone migrate into the newer one. And to do this, an API would include its version number in the resource identifier (i.e., the URL of each resource). This approach makes the version number a mandatory part of the URL to clearly show the version in use.

Another approach, which may not be as clear, is to provide a versionless URL that points to the latest version of the API and an optional URL parameter to overwrite the version. Both approaches have pros and cons that have to be weighted by the developer creating the API. Tables 2-2 and 2-3 show the pros and cons of both options.

Table 2-2. *Pros and Cons of Having the Version of the API As Part of the URL*

Pros	Cons
The version number is clearly visible, helping prevent confusion about the version being used.	URLs are more verbose.
Easy to migrate from one version to another, from a client perspective (all URLs change the same portion—the version number)	A wrong implementation on the API code could cause a huge amount of work when migrating from one version to the other (i.e., if the version is hardcoded on the endpoint's URL template, individually for every endpoint).
Allows cleaner architecture when more than one version of the API needs to be kept working	
Clear and simple migration from one version to the next from the API perspective, since both versions could be kept working in parallel for a period of time, allowing slower clients to migrate without breaking	
The right versioning scheme can make fixes and backward-compatible new features instantly available without the need to update on the client's part.	

Table 2-3. *Pros and Cons of Having the API Version Hidden from the User*

Pros	Cons
Simpler URLs	A Hidden version number might lead to confusion about the version being used.
Instant migration to latest working code of the API	Non-backward-compatible changes will break the clients that are not referencing a specific version of the API.
Simple migration from one version to the next from the client's perspective (only change the value of the attribute)	Complex architecture required to make version selection available
Easy test of client code against the latest version (just don't send version-specific parameters)	

Keeping this in mind, there are several versioning schemes to use when it comes to setting the version of a software product:

- Ubuntu's[7] version numbers represent the year and month of the release; so version 14.04 means it was released in April 2014.

- In the Chromium project, version numbers have four parts:[8] MAJOR. MINOR.BUILD.PATCH. The following is from the Chromium project's page on versioning: MAJOR and MINOR *may* get updated with any significant Google Chrome release (Beta or Stable update). MAJOR *must* get updated for any backward-incompatible user data change (since this data survives updates). BUILD *must* get updated whenever a release candidate is built from the current trunk (at least weekly for Dev channel release candidates). The BUILD number is an ever-increasing number representing a point in time of the Chromium trunk. PATCH *must* get updated whenever a release candidate is built from the BUILD branch.

---

[7]See https://help.ubuntu.com/community/CommonQuestions#Ubuntu_Releases_and_Version_Numbers.
[8]See http://www.chromium.org/developers/version-numbers.

- Another intermediate approach, known as Semantic Versioning or SemVer,[9] is well accepted by the development community. It provides the right amount of information. It has three numbers for each version: MAJOR.MINOR.PATCH.

  - MAJOR represents changes that are not backward-compatible.

  - MINOR represents new features that leave the API backward-compatible.

  - PATCH represents small changes like bug fixes and code optimization.

With that scheme, the first number is the only one that is really relevant to clients, since that'll be the one indicating compatibility with their current version.

By having the latest version of MINOR and PATCH deployed on the API at all times, you're providing clients with the latest compatible features and bug fixes, without making clients update their code.

So with that simple versioning scheme, the endpoints look like this:

```
GET /1/books?limit=10&size=10
POST /v2/photos
GET /books?v=1
```

When choosing a versioning scheme, please take the following into consideration:

- Using the wrong versioning scheme might cause confusion or problems when implementing a client app by consuming the wrong version of the API. For instance, using Ubuntu's versioning scheme for your API might not be the best way to communicate what is going on in each new version.

- The wrong versioning scheme might force clients to update a lot, like when a minor fix is deployed or a new backward-compatible feature is added. Those changes shouldn't require a client update. So don't force the client to specify those parts of the version unless your scheme requires it.

---

[9]See semver.org.

49

Up-to-Date Documentation

No matter how mnemotechnic your endpoints are, you still need to have documentation explaining everything that your API does. Whether optional parameters or the mechanics of an access point, the documentation is fundamental to having a good DX, which translates into more users.

A good API requires more than just a few lines explaining how to use an access point (there is nothing worse than discovering that you need an access point but it has no documentation at all) but needs a full list of parameters and explanatory examples.

Some providers give developers a simple web interface to try their API without having to write any code. This is particularly useful for newcomers.

There are some online services that allow API developers to upload their documentation, as well as those that provide the web UI to test the API; for example, Mashape provides this service for free (see Figure 2-2).

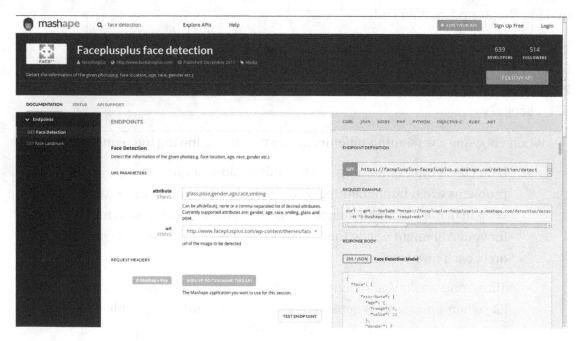

Figure 2-2. *The service provided by Mashape*

Another good example of detailed documentation is at Facebook's developer site.[10] It provides implementation and usage examples for all the platforms that Facebook supports (see Figure 2-3).

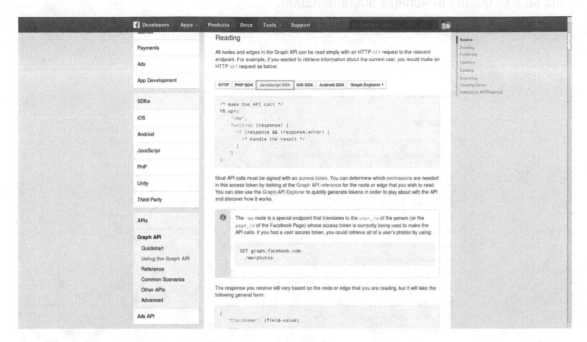

Figure 2-3. *Facebook's API documentation site*

An example of a poorly written documentation is seen in Figure 2-4. It is 4chan's API documentation.[11]

Yes, the API appears to not be complicated enough to merit writing a whole book about it, but then again, there are no examples provided, only a generic explanation of how to find the endpoints and what parameters to use.

Newcomers might find it hard to understand how to implement a simple client that uses this API.

---

[10]See https://developers.facebook.com/docs/graph-api/using-graph-api/v2.1.
[11]See https://github.com/4chan/4chan-API.

Note   It's unfair to compare 4chan's documentation to that of Facebook's, since the size of the teams and companies are completely different. But you should note the lack of quality in 4chan's documentation.

Figure 2-4. *Introduction to 4chan's API documentation*

Although it might not seem like the most productive idea while developing an API, the team needs to consider working on extensive documentation. It is one of the main things that will assure the success or failure of the API for two main reasons:

- It should help newcomers and advance developers to consume your API without any problems.

- It should serve as a blueprint for the development team, if it is kept up-to-date. Jumping into a project mid-development is easier if there is a well-written and well-explained blueprint of how the API is meant to work.

Note   This also applies to updating the documentation when changes are made to the API. You need to keep it updated; otherwise, the effect is the same as not having documentation at all.

Proper Error Handling

Error handling on an API is incredibly important, because if it is done right, it can help the client app understand how to handle errors; and on the human side (the DX), it can help developers understand what it is they're doing wrong and how to fix it.

There are two very distinct moments during the life cycle of an API client that you need to consider error handling:

- *Phase 1*: The development of the client
- *Phase 2*: The client is implemented and being used by end users.

Phase 1: Development of the Client

During the first phase, developers implement the required code to consume the API. It is very likely that a developer will have errors on the requests (things like missing parameters, wrong endpoint names, etc.) during this stage.

Those errors need to be handled properly, which means returning enough information to let developers know what they did wrong and how they can fix it.

A common problem with some systems is that their creators ignore this stage, and when there is a problem with the request, the API crashes, and the returned information is just an error message with the stack trace and the status code 500, as seen in Figure 2-5.

```
                                                        + - View source ⚙
{
    error: "TypeError: Cannot read property 'query' of undefined at BooksHdlr.index
    (/home/fernando/workspace/github/api-design/./handlers/books.js:20:22) at
    ProcessingChain.runChain (/home/fernando/workspace/github/api-
    design/node_modules/vatican/lib/processingChain.js:76:13) at
    /home/fernando/workspace/github/api-
    design/node_modules/vatican/lib/vatican.js:162:36 at
    /home/fernando/workspace/github/api-
    design/node_modules/vatican/lib/defaultRequestParser.js:63:13 at
    Object.module.exports.getBodyContent (/home/fernando/workspace/github/api-
    design/node_modules/vatican/lib/defaultRequestParser.js:20:13) at
    Object.module.exports.parse (/home/fernando/workspace/github/api-
    design/node_modules/vatican/lib/defaultRequestParser.js:57:14) at
    Vatican.parseRequest (/home/fernando/workspace/github/api-
    design/node_modules/vatican/lib/vatican.js:82:24) at Vatican.requestHandler
    (/home/fernando/workspace/github/api-
    design/node_modules/vatican/lib/vatican.js:154:18) at Server.EventEmitter.emit
    (events.js:98:17) at HTTPParser.parser.onIncoming (http.js:2108:12)"
}
```

Figure 2-5. *A classic example of a crash on the API returning the stack trace*

The response in Figure 2-5 shows what happens when you forget to add error handling in the client development stage. The stack trace returned might give the developer some sort of clue (at best) as to what exactly went wrong, but it also shows a lot of unnecessary information, so it ends up being confusing. This certainly hurts development time, and no doubt would be a major point against the DX of the API.

On the other hand, let's take a look at a proper error response for the same error in Figure 2-6.

```
{
    error: true,
    error_msg: "Missing parameter "key" from querystring, please add it with the value
    you got from the development console on our site.",
    error_code: 4
}
```

Figure 2-6. *A proper error response would look like this*

Figure 2-6 clearly shows that there has been an error, what the error is, and an error code. The response only has three attributes, but they're all helpful:

- The error indicator gives the developer a clear way to check whether or not the response is an error message (you could also check against the status code of the response).

- The error message is clearly intended for the developer and not only states what's missing, but also explains how to fix it.

- A custom error code, if explained in the documentation, could help a developer automate actions when this type of response happens again.

Phase 2: The Client Is Implemented and Being Used by End Users

During this stage in the life cycle of the client, you're not expecting any more developer errors, such as using the wrong endpoint, missing parameters, and the like, but there could still be problems caused by the data generated by the user.

Client applications that request some kind of input from the user are always subject to errors on the user's part, and even though there are always ways to validate that input before it reaches the API layer, it's not safe to assume all clients will do that. So the safest bet for any API designer and developer is to assume there is no validation done by the client, and anything that could go wrong with the data will go wrong. This is also a safe assumption to make from a security point of view, so it's providing a minor security improvement as a side effect.

With that mindset, the API implemented should be rock-solid and able to handle any type of errors in the input data.

The response should mimic that from phase 1: there should be an error indicator, an error message stating what's wrong (and, if possible, how to fix it), and a custom error code. The custom error code is especially useful in this stage, since it'll provide the client with the ability to customize the error shown to the end user (even showing a different but still relevant error message).

Multiple SDK / Libraries

If you expect your API to be massively used across different technologies and platforms, it might be a good idea to develop and provide support for libraries and SDKs that can be used with your system.

By doing so, you provide developers with the means to consume your services, so all they have to do is use these services to create their client apps. Essentially, you're shaving off potential weeks or months (depending on the size of your system) of development time.

Another benefit is that most developers will inherently trust your libraries over others that do the same, because you're the owner of the service those libraries are consuming.

Finally, consider open sourcing the code of your libraries. These days, the open source community is thriving. Developers will undoubtedly help maintain and improve your libraries if they're of use to them.

Let's look again at some of the biggest APIs out there:

- Facebook API provides SDKs for iOS, Android, JavaScript, PHP, and Unity.[12]

- Google Maps API provides SDKs for several technologies, including iOS, the Web, and Android.[13]

---

[12]See `https://developers.facebook.com` (see the bottom of the page for the list of SDKs).
[13]See `https://developers.google.com/maps/`.

- Twitter API provides SDKs for several of their APIs, including Java, ASP, C++, Clojure, .NET, Go, JavaScript, and a lot of other languages.[14]

- Amazon provides SDKs for their AWS service, including PHP, Ruby, .NET, and iOS. They even have those SDKs on GitHub for anyone to see.[15]

Security

Securing your API is a very important step in the development process, and it should not be ignored, unless what you're building is small enough and has no sensitive data to merit the effort.

There are two big security issues to deal with when designing an API:

- *Authentication*: Who's going to access the API?

- *Authorization*: What will they be able to access once logged in?

Authentication deals with letting valid users access the features provided by the API. Authorization deals with handling what those authenticated users can actually do inside the system.

Before going into details about each specific issue, there are some common aspects that need to be remembered when dealing with security on RESTful systems (at least, those based on HTTP):

- *RESTful systems are meant to be stateless*: Remember that REST defines the server as stateless, which means that storing the user data in session after the initial login is not a good idea (if you want to stay within the guidelines provided by REST, that is).

- *Remember to use HTTPS:* On RESTful systems based on HTTP, HTTPS should be used to assure encryption of the channel, making it harder to capture and read data traffic (man-in-the-middle attack).

---

[14]See https://dev.twitter.com/overview/api/twitter-libraries.
[15]See https://github.com/aws.

Accessing the System

There are some widely used authentication schemes out there meant to provide different levels of security when signing users into a system. Some of the most commonly known are Basic Auth with TSL, Digest Auth, OAuth 1.0a, and OAuth 2.0.

I'll go over these and talk about each of their pros and cons. I'll also cover an alternative method that should prove to be the most RESTful, in the sense that it's 100% stateless.

Almost Stateless Methods

OAuth 1.0a, OAuth 2.0, Digest Auth, and Basic Auth + TSL are the go-to methods of authentication these days. They work wonderfully, they have been implemented in all of the modern programming languages, and they have proven to be the right choice for the job (when used for the right use-case). That being said, as you're about to see, none of them are 100% stateless.

They all depend on having the user have information stored on some kind of cache layer on the server side. This little detail, especially for the purists out there, means a no-go when designing a RESTful system, because it goes against one of the most basic of the constraints imposed by REST: *Communication between client and server must be stateless.*

This means the state of the user should not be stored anywhere.

You will look the other way in this particular case, however. I'll cover the basics of each method anyway, because in real life, you have to compromise and you have to find a balance between purism and practicality. But don't worry. I'll go over an alternative design that will solve authentication and stay true to REST.

Basic Auth with TSL

Thanks to the fact that you're basing REST on HTTP for the purpose of this book, the latter provides a basic authentication method that most of the languages can support.

Keep in mind, though, that this method is aptly named, since it's quite basic and works by sending the username and password unencrypted over HTTP. So the only way to make it secure is to use it with a secured connection over HTTPS (HTTP + TSL).

This authentication method works as follows (see Figure 2-7):

1. First, a client makes a request for a resource without any special header.

2. The server responds with a 401 unauthorized response, and within it, a WWW-Authenticate header, specifying the method to use (Basic or Digest) and the realm name.

3. The client then sends the same request but adds the Authorization header, with the string USERNAME:PASSWORD encoded in base 64.

On the server side, there needs to be some code to decode the authentication string and load the user data from the session storage used (normally a database).

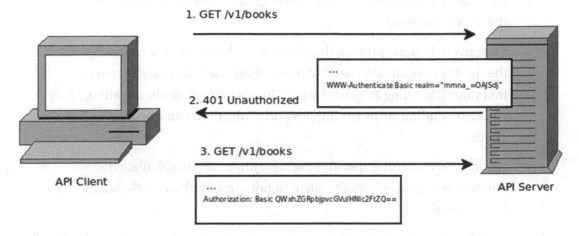

Figure 2-7. *The steps between client and server on Basic Auth*

Aside from the fact that this approach is one of the many that will break the nonstateless constraint, it's easy and fast to implement.

Note   When using this method, if the password for a logged in user is reset, then the login data sent on the request becomes old and the current session is terminated.

Digest Auth

This method is an improvement over the previous one, in the sense that it adds an extra layer of security by encrypting the login information. The communication with the server works the same way, by sending the same headers back and forth.

With this methodology, upon receiving a request for a protected resource, the server will respond with a WWW-Authenticate header and some specific parameters. Here are some of the most interesting:

- *Nounce*: A uniquely generated string. This string needs to be unique on every 401 response.

- *Opaque*: A string returned by the server that has to be sent back by the client unaltered

- *Qop*: Even though optional, this parameter should be sent to specify the quality of protection needed (more than one token can be sent in this value). Sending auth back would imply a simple authentication, whereas sending auth-int implies authentication with integrity check.

- *Algorithm*: This string specifies the algorithm used to calculate the checksum response from the client. If not present, then MD5 should be assumed.

For the full list of parameters and implementation details, please refer to the RFC.[16] Here is a list of some of the most interesting ones:

- *Username*: The unencrypted username.

- *URI*: The URI you're trying to access.

- *Response*: The encrypted portion of the response. This proves that you are who you say you are.

- *Qop*: If present, it should be one of the supported values sent by the server.

---

[16]See https://www.ietf.org/rfc/rfc2617.txt.

To calculate the response, the following logic needs to be applied:

`MD5(HA1:STRING:HA2)`

Those values for HA1 are calculated as follows:

- If no algorithm is specified on the response, then
  `MD5(username:realm:password)` should be used.

- If the algorithm is MD5-less, then it should be
  `MD5(MD5(username:realm:password):nonce:cnonce)`

Those values for HA2 are calculated as follows:

- If qop is auth, then `MD5(method:digestURI)` should be used.

- If qop is auth-int, then `MD5(method:digestURI:MD5(entityBody))`
  should be used.

Finally, the response will be as follows:

`MD5(HA1:nonce:nonceCount:clientNonce:HA2) //for the case when "qop" is`
`"auth" or "auth-int"`
`MD5(HA1:nonce:HA2) //when "qop" is unspecified.`

The main issue with this method is that the encryption used is based on MD5, and in 2004 it was proven that this algorithm is not collision-resistant, which basically means a man-in-the-middle attack would make it possible for an attacker to get the necessary information and generate a set of valid credentials.

A possible improvement over this method, just like with its "Basic" brother, would be adding TSL; this would definitely help make it more secure.

OAuth 1.0a

OAuth 1.0a is the most secure of the four nonstateless methodologies described in this section. The process is a bit more tedious than the ones described earlier (see Figure 2-8), but the trade-off here is a significantly increased level of security.

In this case, the service provider has to allow the developer of the client app to register the app on the provider's web site. By doing so, the developer obtains a consumer key (a unique identifying key for his application) and the consumer secret. Once that process is done, the following steps are required:

1. The client app needs a request token. The purpose is to receive the user's approval and then request an access token. To get the request token, a specific URL must be provided by the server; in this step, the consumer key and the consumer secret are used.

2. Once the request token is obtained, the client must make a request using the token on a specific server URL (i.e., `http://provider.com/oauth/authorize`) to get authorization from the end user.

3. After authorization from the user is given, then the client app makes a request to the provider for an access token and a token secret key.

4. Once the access token and secret token are obtained, the client app is able to request protected resources for the provider on behalf of the user by signing each request.

Figure 2-8. *The interaction between client and server*

For more details on how this method works, please refer to the complete documentation.[17]

OAuth 2.0

OAuth 2.0 is meant to be the evolution of OAuth 1.0a; it focuses on client developer simplicity. The main problem with implementations of systems that worked with OAuth 1.0 was the complexity implied in the last step: signing every request.

Due to its complexity, the last step is the key weak point of the algorithm: if either the client or server makes a tiny mistake, then the requests will not validate. Even when the same aspect made it the only methodology that didn't need to work on top of SSL (or TSL), this benefit wasn't enough.

OAuth 2.0 tries to simplify the last step by making some key changes, mainly:

- It relies on SSL (or TSL) to ensure that the information sent back and forth is encrypted.

- Signatures are not required for requests after the token has been generated.

To summarize, this version of OAuth tries to simplify the complexity introduced by OAuth 1.0, while sacrificing security at the same time (by relying on TSL to ensure data encryption). It is the preferred method over OAuth 1.0 if the devices you're dealing with have support for TSL (computers, mobile devices, etc.); otherwise, you might want to consider using other options.

A Stateless Alternative

As you've seen, the alternatives you have when it comes to implementing a security protocol to allow users to sign into a RESTful API are not stateless, and even though you should be prepared to make that commitment to gain the benefits of tried and tested ways of securing your application, there is a fully REST compatible way of doing it as well.

If you go back to Chapter 1, the stateless constraints basically imply that any and all states of the communication between client and server should be included on every request made by the client. This of course includes the user information, so if you want to have stateless authentication, then you need to include that in your requests as well.

---

[17]See http://oauth.net/core/1.0a/.

If you want to ensure the authenticity of each request, you can borrow the signature step of OAuth 1.0a and apply it on every request by using a pre-established secret key between the client and the server and a MAC (Message Authentication Code) algorithm to do the signing (see Figure 2-9).

As you're keeping it stateless, the information required to generate the MAC needs to also be sent as part of the request, so the server can re-create the result and corroborate its validity.

This approach has some clear advantages in our case, mainly:

- It's simpler than both OAuth 1.0a and OAuth 2.0.

- Zero storage is needed, since any and all required information to validate the encryption needs to be sent on every request.

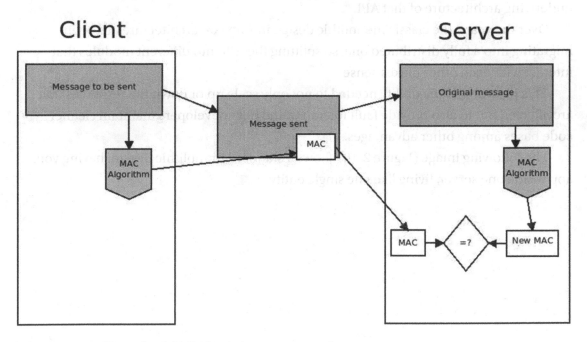

Figure 2-9. *How the MAC signing process works*

Scalability

Last but certainly not least is *scalability*.

Scalability is usually an underestimated aspect of API design, mainly because it's quite difficult to fully understand and predict the reach one API will have before it launches. It might be easier to estimate this if the team has previous experience with similar projects (e.g., Google has probably gotten quite good at calculating their scalability for new APIs before launch day), but if it's their first one, then it might not be as easy.

A good API should be able to scale—that means it should be able to handle as much traffic as it gets without compromising its performance. But it also means it should not spend resources if they're not needed. This is not only a reflection of the hardware on which the API resides (although that is an important aspect), but also a reflection of the underlying architecture of that API.

Over the years, the classic monolithic design in software architecture has been migrating into a fully distributed one, so splitting the API into different modules that interact with each other makes sense.

This provides the flexibility needed to not only scale up or down the resources that are affected but to also provide fault tolerance and help developers maintain cleaner code bases among other advantages.

The following image (Figure 2-10) shows a standard monolithic design, having your app inside one server, living like one single entity.

The Internet

Figure 2-10. *Simple diagram of a monolithic architecture*

In Figure 2-11 you see a distributed design. If compared with Figure 2-10, you can see where the advantages come from (better resource usage, fault tolerance, easier to scale up or down, etc.).

Figure 2-11. *A diagram showing an example of a distributed architecture*

Achieving a distributed architecture to ensure scalability using REST is quite simple. Fielding's paper proposes a distributed system based on a client–server scheme.

So splitting the entire system into a set of smaller APIs and having them talk to each other when required will ensure the advantages mentioned earlier.

For instance, let's look at an internal system for a bookstore (Table 2-4).

Table 2-4. *List of Entities and Their Role Inside the System*

Entity	Description
Books	Represents the inventory of the store. It'll control everything from book data, to number of copies, and so forth.
Clients	Contact information of clients
Users	Internal bookstore users; they will have access to the system
Purchases	Records information about book sales

Now, consider that system on a small bookstore, one that is just starting and has just a few employees. It's very tempting to go with a monolithic design; not a lot of resources will be spent and the design is quite simple.

Now, consider what would happen if the small bookstore suddenly grows so much that it expands into several other bookstores. They go from having 1 store to 100, employee numbers grow, books need better tracking, and purchases skyrocket.

The simple system from before will not be enough to handle such growth. It would require changes to support networking, centralized data storage, distributed access, better storage capacity, and so forth. In other words, scaling it up would be too expensive and probably would require a complete rewrite.

Finally, consider an alternative beginning. What if you took the time to create the first system using a distributed architecture based on REST? With each sub-system being a different API and having them all talk to each other.

Then you would've been able to scale the whole thing much easier; working independently on each sub-system there would be no need for full rewrites and the system could potentially keep growing to meet new needs.

Summary

This chapter covered what the developer community considers a "good API," which means the following:

- Remembering the Developer eXperience (DX).

- Being able to grow and improve without breaking existing clients

- Having up-to-date documentation

- Providing correct error handling

- Providing multiple SDK and libraries

- Thinking about security

- Being able to scale, both up and down, as needed

In the next chapter, you'll learn why Node.js is a perfect match for implementing everything you've learned in this chapter.

CHAPTER 3

Node.js and REST

There are currently too many technologies out there—be it programming languages, platforms, or frameworks. Why is it, then, that Node.js—a project that's hasn't even reached version 1.0 at the time of this writing—is so popular these days?

Advances in hardware make it possible for developers to focus less on hyper-optimizing their code to gain speed, allowing them to focus more on speed of development; thus, a new set of tools has surfaced.

These tools make it easier for novice developers to develop new projects, while at the same time provide advanced developers with access to the same type of power they got with the old tools. These tools are the new programming languages and frameworks of today (Ruby on Rails, Laravel, Symfony, Express.js, Node.js, Django, and much more).

In this chapter, I'll go over one of the newest of these: Node.js. It was created in 2009 by Ryan Dahl and sponsored by Joyent, the company for which Dahl worked. At its core, Node.js[1] utilizes the Google V8[2] engine to execute JavaScript code on the server side. I'll cover its main features to help you understand why it is such a great tool for API development.

The following are some of the aspects of Node.js covered in this chapter:

- *Async programming*: This is a great feature of Node.js. I'll discuss how you can leverage it to gain better results than if using other technologies.

- *Async I/O*: Although related to async programming, this deserves a separate mention because in input/output-heavy applications, this particular feature presents the winning card for choosing Node.js over other technologies.

---

[1]See http://en.wikipedia.org/wiki/Node.js.
[2]See http://en.wikipedia.org/wiki/V8_(JavaScript_engine).

© Fernando Doglio 2018
F. Doglio, *REST API Development with Node.js*, https://doi.org/10.1007/978-1-4842-3715-1_3

- *Simplicity*: Node.js makes getting started and writing your first web server very easy. You'll see some examples.

- *Amazing integration with JSON-based services* (like other APIs, MongoDB, etc.).

- *The community and the Node package manager* (npm): I'll go over the benefits of having a huge community of developers using the technology and how npm has helped.

- *Who's using it?*: Finally, I'll quickly go over some of the big companies using Node.js in their production platforms.

Asynchronous Programming

Asynchronous (or async) programming is perhaps at the same time one of the best and most confusing features of Node.js.

Asynchronous programming means that for every asynchronous function that you execute, you can't expect it to return the results before moving forward with the program's flow. Instead, you'll need to provide a callback block/function that will be executed once the asynchronous code finishes.

Figure 3-1 shows a regular, non-asynchronous flow.

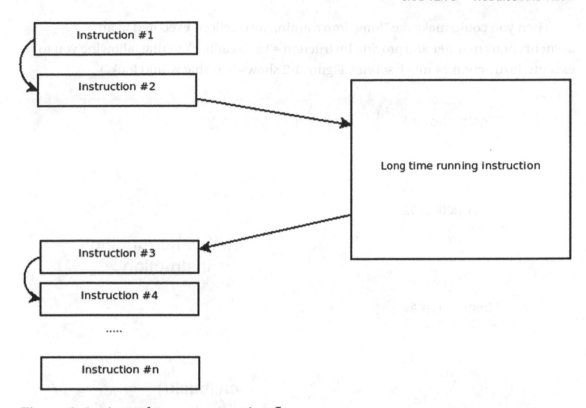

Figure 3-1. *A synchronous execution flow*

Figure 3-1 represents a set of instructions that run in a synchronous manner. To execute Instruction #4, you need to wait as long as the "long time running instruction" takes and then wait for Instruction #3 to finish. But what if Instruction #4 and Instruction #3 weren't really related? What if you didn't really mind in which order Instruction #3 and Instruction #4 executed in relationship to each other?

Then you could make the "long time running instruction" executed in an asynchronous manner and provide Instruction #3 as a callback to that, allowing you to execute Instruction #4 much sooner. Figure 3-2 shows how that would look.

Figure 3-2. *An asynchronous execution flow*

Instead of waiting for it to finish, Instruction #4 is executed right after Instruction #2 starts the asynchronous "long time running instruction."

This is a very simple example of the potential benefits of asynchronous programming. Sadly, like with most in this digital world, nothing comes without a price, and the added benefits also come with a nasty trade-off: debugging asynchronous code can be a real head-breaker.

Developers are trained to think of their code in the sequential way they write it, so debugging a code that is not sequential can be difficult to newcomers.

For instance, Listings 3-1 and 3-2 show the same piece of code written in a synchronous and an asynchronous manner, respectively.

Listing 3-1. Synchronous Version of a Simple Read File Operation

```
console.log("About to read the file... ")
let content = fs.readFileSync("/path/to/file")
console.log("File content: ", content)
```

Listing 3-2. Asynchronous Version of a Simple File Read Operation with a Common Mistake

```
console.log("About to read the file...")
let content = ""
fs.readFile("/path/to/file", function(err, data) {
   content = data
})
console.log("File content: ", content)
```

If you haven't guessed it yet, Listing 3-2 will print the following:

```
File content:
```

and the reason for that is directly related to the diagram shown in Figure 3-3. Let's use it to see what's going on with the buggy asynchronous version.

Figure 3-3. *The error from Listing 3-2*

It's pretty clear why the content of the file is not being written: the callback is being executed after the last console.log line. This is a very common mistake by new developers, not only with Node.js, but more specifically with AJAX calls on the front end. They set up their code in a way to use the content returned by the asynchronous call before it actually ends.

To finish the example, Listing 3-3 shows how the code needs to be written to properly work.

Listing 3-3. Correct Version of the Asynchronous File Read Operation

```
console.log("About to read the file...")
let content = ""
fs.readFile("/path/to/file", function(err, data) {
    content = data
    console.log("File content: ", content)
})
```

Simple. You just moved the last console.log line into the callback function, so you're sure that the content variable is set correctly.

Async Advanced

Asynchronous programming is not just about making sure that you set up the callback function correctly, it also allows for some interesting flow control patterns that can be used to improve the efficiency of the app.

Let's look at two distinct and very useful control flow patterns for asynchronous programming: *parallel flow* and *serial flow*.

Parallel Flow

The idea behind parallel flow is that the program can run a set of nonrelated tasks in parallel but only call the callback function provided (to gather their collective outputs) after all tasks have finished executing.

Basically, Listing 3-4 shows what you want.

Listing 3-4. Signature of the Parallel Function

```
//functionX symbols are references to individual functions
parallel([function1, function2, function3, function4], data => {
   ///do something with the combined output once they all finished
})
```

To know when each of the functions passed in the array have finished execution, they'll have to execute a callback function with the results of their operation. The callback will be the only attribute they receive. Listing 3-5 shows the parallel function.

Listing 3-5. Implementation of the Parallel Function

```
function parallel(funcs, callback) {
  var results = [],
      callsToCallback = 0

  funcs.forEach( fn => { // iterate over all functions
    setTimeout(fn(done), 200) // and call them with a 200 ms delay
  })

  function done(data) { // the functions will call this one when they
  finish and they'll pass the results here
    results.push(data)
    if(++callsToCallback == funcs.length) {
       callback(results)
    }
  }
}
```

The implementation in Listing 3-5 is very simple, but it fulfills its task: it runs a set of functions in a parallel way (you'll see that since Node.js runs in a single thread, true parallelism is not possible, so this is as close as you can get).

This type of control flow is particularly useful when dealing with calls to external services.

Let's look at a practical example. Assume your API needs to do several operations that, although aren't related to each other, need to happen before the user can see the results. For instance, load the list of books from the database, query an external service to get news about new books out this week, and log the request into a file. If you were to execute all of those tasks in a series (see Listing 3-6), waiting for one to finish before the next one can be run, then the user would most probably suffer a delay on the response because the total time needed for the execution is the sum of all individual times.

But if instead you can execute all of them in parallel (see Listing 3-7), then the total time is actually equal to the time it takes the slowest task to execute.[3]

Let's look at both cases in Listings 3-6 and 3-7.

Listing 3-6. Example of a Serial Flow (takes longer)

```
//request handling code...
//assume "db" is already initialized and provides an interface to the data base

db.query("books", {limit:1000, page: 1}, books => {
    services.bookNews.getThisWeeksNews(news => {
        services.logging.logRequest(request, () => { //nothing returned, but
        you need to call it so you know the logging finished
            response.render({listOfBooks: books, bookNews: news})
        })
    })
})
```

Listing 3-7. Example of a Parallel Execution Flow

```
//request handling code...

 parallel([
    callback => { db.query("books", {limit: 1000, page: 1}, callback) },
    callback => { services.bookNews.getThisWeeksNews(callback) },
    callback => { services.logRequest(request, callback) }
 ], data => {
        var books = findData("books", data)
```

---

[3]This is a rough approximation, since the time added by the parallel function needs to be taken into account for an exact number.

```
    var news = findData("news", data)
    response.render({listOfBooks: books, bookNews: news})
})
```

Listings 3-6 and 3-7 show how each approach looks. The findData function simply looks into the data array and, based on the structure of the items, returns the desired one (first parameter). In the implementation of parallel a function such as findData is needed because you can't be sure in which order the functions finished and then sent back their results.

Aside from the clear speed boost that the code gets, it's also easier to read and easier to add new tasks to the parallel flow—just add a new item to the array.

Serial Flow

The serial flow provides the means to easily specify a list of functions that need to be executed in a particular order. This solution doesn't provide a speed boost like parallel flow does, but it does provide the ability to write such code and keep it clean, staying away from what is normally known as *spaghetti code*.

Listing 3-8 shows what you should try to accomplish.

Listing 3-8. Signature of the Serial Function

```
serial([
 function1, function2, function3
], data => {
    //do something with the combined results
})
```

Listing 3-9 shows what you shouldn't do.

Listing 3-9. Example of a Common Case of Nested Callbacks

```
function1(data1 => {
   function2(data2 => {
      function3(data3 => {
        //do something with all the output
      }
   }
}
```

You can see how the code in Listing 3-9 could get out of hand if the number of functions kept growing. So the serial approach helps keep the code organized and readable.

Let's look at a possible implementation of the serial function in Listing 3-10.

Listing 3-10. Implementation of the Serial Function

```
function serial(functions, done) {
  let fn = functions.shift() //get the first function off the list
  let results = []
  fn(next)
  function next(result) {
      results.push(result) //save the results to be passed into the final
      callback once you don't have any more functions to execute.
      let nextFn = functions.shift()
      if (nextFn) nextFn(next)
      else done(results)
  }
}
```

There are more variations to these functions, like using an error parameter to handle errors automatically or limiting the number of simultaneous functions in the parallel flow.

All in all, asynchronous programming brings a lot of benefits to implementing APIs. Parallel workflow comes in very handy when dealing with external services, which normally any API would deal with—for instance, database access, other APIs, disk I/O, and so forth. And at the same time, the serial workflow is useful when implementing things like Express.js middleware.[4]

For a fully functional and tested library that thrives on asynchronous programming, please check out async.js.[5]

---

[4]See http://expressjs.com/guide/using-middleware.html.
[5]See https://github.com/caolan/async.

Asynchronous I/O

A specific case of asynchronous programming relates to a very interesting feature provided by Node.js: asynchronous I/O.

This feature is highly relevant to the internal architecture of Node.js. As I've said, Node.js doesn't provide multi-threading; it actually works with a single thread that runs an event loop.

Essentially, the Event Loop works on phases; for every tick of the loop, it goes through a new phase. For every phase, it keeps a FIFO queue of callbacks, and it executes as many callbacks in that phase as it can (there is a limit to how many callbacks can be called on every tick).

There is a common misconception that the event loops handles all asynchronous functions with threads from Libuv (the library V8 uses to handle asynchronism). But it's not exactly true; these threads are only used in special cases when there is no other way, because modern OS and other systems, such as Databases, already provide asynchronous interfaces, so the engine will try to use them, and if there is no async alternative, it'll resort to the thread pool.

The aforementioned phases are:

1. Timers: Here is where setTimeout and setInterval are evaluated.

2. Callbacks: Here is where system-specific callbacks are executed.

3. Poll: This is where I/O-related callbacks get executed, as long as there are any. Once all callbacks have been executed (or the system's limit is reached), if there is nothing else to execute, then the engine will wait for new callbacks to be registered in this phase to execute them.

4. Check: Here is where setImmediate is evaluated.

5. Close events: Here is where the callbacks registered for the 'close' events are executed.

If you wanted to, there is a very interesting way to look into this and test it on your own. Simply by using the following code, you'll see how the execution is done internally:

Listing 3-11. Example showing the different phases for the event loop

```
const request = require("request"),
        fibonacci = require("fibonacci"),
        fs = require("fs");

process.nextTick(() => {
        process.stdout.write("NT #1\n");
});

fs.readFile("./index.js",  (err, data) => {
        process.stdout.write("1: I/O Polling...\n");
});

request.get("http://google.com", (err, res, body) => {
        process.stdout.write("2: System polling...\n");
})

setImmediate(() => {
        process.stdout.write("3: Set Immediate phase...\n");
});

setTimeout(() => {
        process.stdout.write("4: Timers...\n");
}, 0);

process.stdout.write("5: Fibonacci(20): " + fibonacci.iterate(20).number +
" -Callback\n");

process.nextTick(() => {
        process.stdout.write("NT #2\n");
})
```

The result from executing the code from Listing 3-11 is the following (note that this is in my computer, with Node version 8.1.3; results might vary on your side, but they should be similar nonetheless):

1. 5: Fibonacci(20): 6765 callback

2. NT #1

3. NT #2

4.   4: Timers...

5.   3: Set Immediate phase...

6.   1: I/O Polling...

7.   2: System polling...

From these results, we can extrapolate the following behavior:

1.   The first thing to get executed (and resolved) is the current thread, which means the line of the fibonacci call. The rest of the lines were executed, but they have not yet resolved, because they're all different forms of asynchronous behavior.

2.   After the current phase is over, the event loop tries to move to the next one, but first it needs to call the nextTick method, which is executed on a separate queue. This means that no matter what the current phase is, it'll resolve all callbacks you've defined and then move to the next phase.

3.   By this time, the Poll phase has probably run, and it has verified that no callback has been registered for it yet (because the file is still being read and the HTTP Request is still being made), so it continues to the timers and check phases.

4.   In this case, depending on the performance of your system, either one of them can run. The point here is that since we've setup the timeout for `setTimeout` to 0, the execution of that callback and the one for `setImmediate` is non-deterministic. In other words, you won't be able to predict their order of execution.[6]

5.   Finally, after the timers have run, the only thing missing is to wait on the Poll phase until the I/O operations end, and given the nature of them, reading the file will end first, leaving the HTTP request to be resolved in the last place.

---

[6]See Node.js' official documentation about this: `https://nodejs.org/en/docs/guides/event-loop-timers-and-nexttick/#process-nexttick-vs-setimmediate`

Figure 3-4 attempts to present a graphical representation of the preceding events, starting from what would be step 3.

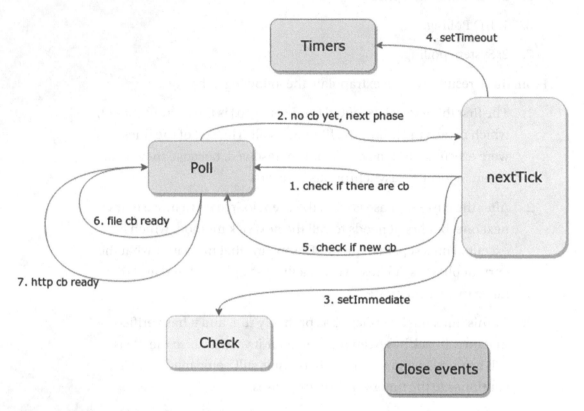

Figure 3-4. *Graphical representation of how the event loop would work for the code of listing 3-11*

You can read more on the how the event loop works from the official documentation, but this should give you a basic idea of how it should work. You can tweak and change the code sample from Listing 3-11 to see how the results change until you're sure there is no witchcraft involved. (I know it took me several attempts to get there.)

Async I/O vs. Sync I/O

Finally, for the sake of proving that everything I've stated so far is true and that Node.js works best using async I/O, I've done some very simple benchmarking. I've created a simple API with two endpoints:

- /async: This reads a 1.6MB file asynchronously before returning a simple JSON response.

- /sync: This reads a 1.6MB file synchronously before returning a simple JSON response.

Both endpoints do exactly the same, only in a different manner (see Listing 3-11). The idea is to prove that even in such simple code, the event loop can handle multiple requests better when the underlying code makes use of the asynchronous I/O provided by the platform.

Listing 3-12 is the code of both endpoints; the API was written using Vatican.js.[7]

Listing 3-12. Example of Two Endpoints Coded Using the Express.js Framework

```
//Async handler
const fs = require("fs")
class AsyncHdlr {
        constructor() {
        }
        @endpoint(url: /async method: get)
        index(req, res, next) {
                let fname = __dirname + "/file.txt";
                fs.appendFile(fname, Date.now(), (err, content) => {
                        res.send({
                           success: true
                        })
                })
        }
}
```

---

[7]See https://www.npmjs.com/package/vatican

```
module.exports = AsyncHdlr;

//Sync handler
const fs = require("fs")

class SyncHdlr {

        constructor() {
        }
        @endpoint(url: /sync method: get)
        index(req, res, next) {
                let fname = __dirname + "/file.txt";
                fs.appendFileSync(fname, Date.now());
            res.send({
                    success: true
            });
        }
}

module.exports = SyncHdlr;
```

The benchmark was done using the Apache Benchmark[8] tool using the following parameters:

- Number of requests: 10,000

- Concurrent requests: 100

---

[8]See http://httpd.apache.org/docs/2.2/programs/ab.html.

The results are shown in Table 3-1.

Table 3-1. *Results from the Benchmark of the Two Endpoints Shown in Listing 3-11*

Synchronous Endpoint	Asynchronous Endpoint
Requests per second: 3065.00[#/sec.] (mean)	Requests per second: 3877.82 [#/sec.] (mean)
Time per request 32.4626 [ms] (mean)	***Time per request: 25.788 [ms] (mean)***
Time per request: 0.326 [ms] (mean, across all concurrent requests)	Time per request: 0.258 [ms] (mean, across all concurrent requests)
Transfer rate: 652.51 [KBps] received	Transfer rate: 825.55 [KBps] received

As you can see in Table 3-1, for even the simplest of examples, there are 812 more requests being served by the asynchronous code than in the synchronous code in the same amount of time. Another interesting item is that each request is almost 8 milliseconds faster on the asynchronous endpoint; this might not be a huge number, but considering the nonexistent complexity of the code you're using, it's quite relevant.

Simplicity

Node.js (more specifically, JavaScript) is not a complicated language. It follows the basic principles that similar scripting languages follow (like Ruby, Python, and PHP), but with a twist (like all of them do). Node.js is simple enough for any developer to pick up and start coding in no time, and yet it's powerful enough to achieve almost anything developers can set their minds to.

Although JavaScript is an amazing language, and a focus of this book, like I've said and will keep saying: there are no silver bullets when it comes to programming. JavaScript has gained a lot of traction over the years, but it has also gained a lot of haters, and they have their very valid reasons: a nonstandard object-oriented model, weird usage of the "this" keyword, a lack of functionality built into the language (it has a lot of libraries dedicated to implementing basic features that come built-in in other languages), and the list goes on. In the end, every tool needs to be chosen based on its strengths. Node.js is a particularly strong option for developing APIs, as you're about to see.

Node.js adds a certain useful flavor to the language, simplifying a developer's life when trying to develop back-end code. It not only adds the required utilities to work with I/O (which front-end JavaScript doesn't have for obvious security reasons), but it also provides stability for all the different flavors of JavaScript that each web browser supports.

One example of this is how easy it is to set up a web server with just a few lines of code. Let's look at that in Listing 3-13.

Listing 3-13. Simple Example of a Web Server Written in Node.js

```
const http = require("http")
 http.createServer((req, res) =>  { //create the server
//request handler code here
 });
 http.listen(3000) //start it up on port 3000
```

JavaScript also has the advantage of being the standard front-end language for all commercial web browsers, which means that if you're a web developer with front-end experience, you have certainly come across JavaScript.

This makes it simpler for the developer who's migrating from the front end into the back end; since the language basics haven't changed, you only need to learn about the new things and change into a back-end mindset. At the same time, this helps companies find Node.js developers faster.

With all that in mind, let's look at some of the main characteristics of JavaScript that make it such a simple (and yet powerful) option.

Dynamic Typing

Dynamic typing is a basic characteristic present in most common languages nowadays, but it's no less powerful because of that. This little feature allows the developer to not have to think too much when declaring a variable; just give it a name and move on.

Listing 3-14 shows something you can't do with a statically typed language.

Listing 3-14. Example of Code Taking Advantage Of Dynamic Typing

```
var a, b, tmp //declare the variables (just give them names)

//initialize them with different types
a = 10
b = "hello world"
//now swap the values
tmp = a
```

```
a = b //even with automatic casting, a language like C won't be able to
        cast "hello world" into an integer value
b = tmp
console.log(a) //prints "hello world"
console.log(b) //prints 10
```

Object-Oriented Programming Simplified

JavaScript it not an object-oriented language, but it does have support for some of these features (see Listing 3-14 and Listing 3-16). You'll have enough access to objects to conceptualize problems and solutions using them, which is always a very intuitive way of thinking, but at the same time, you're not dealing with concepts like polymorphism, interfaces, or others that, despite helping to structure code, have proven to be dispensable when designing applications.

Listing 3-15. Simplified Object Orientation Example

```
var myObject = { //JS object notation helps simplify definitions
        myAttribute: "some value",
        myMethod: function(param1, param2) {
                //does something here
        }
}
//And the just...
myObject.myMethod(...)
```

Whereas with other languages, like Java (a strongly object-oriented language), you would have to do what's shown in Listing 3-16.

Listing 3-16. Example of a Class Definition in Java

```
class myClass {
        public string myAttribute;
        public  myClass() {
        }
        public void myMethod(int param1, int param2) {
                //does something here
        }
}
```

```
//And then
myClass myObj = new myClass();
myObj.myMethod(...);
```

Much less verbose, isn't it?

In Listing 3-17, let's look at another example of the powerful object orientation that you have available.

Listing 3-17. Another Example of the Features Provided by Object Orientation in JavaScript

```
var aDog = { //behave like a dog
        makeNoise: function() {
                console.log("woof!");
        }
}
var aCat = { //behave like a cat
        makeNoise: function() {
                console.log("Meewww!");
        }
}
var myAnimal = { //our main object
        makeNoise: function() {
                console.log("cri... cri....")
        },
        speak: function() {
                this.makeNoise()
        }

}
myAnimal.speak() //no change, so.. crickets!
myAnimal.speak.apply(aDog) //this will print "woof!"
//switch behavior
myAnimal.speak.apply(aCat) //this will now print "Meewww!"
```

You were able to encapsulate a simple behavior into an object and pass it into another object to automatically overwrite its default behavior. That's something that's built into the language; you didn't have to write any specific code to achieve this feature.

The new Class construct from ES6

Tired of being laughed at and pointed at for not having a proper class construct for the OOP lovers, the good folks at Ecma International decided to create one. Actually, I'm just guessing, I don't know why they decided to add it, but they did, so be happy about it or don't, your call.

The point is: if you like solving your problems using OOP, now you have the most basic structure any OOP language provides, right at your fingertips. But don't get too excited just yet, they're not the same kind of classes you'd have in JAVA or any other fully OOP language. No, they're just your basic, nothing-fancy type of classes, and let me explain with the following code sample:

Listing 3-18. Example of Classes in ES6

```
"use strict";
class AnotherClass {

        constructor(p1, p2) {
                this._param1 = p1;
                this._param2 = p2;
        }

}

class SampleClass extends AnotherClass {

        constructor(param1, param2) {
                super(param1, param2)
        }

        set param1(val) {
                this._param1 = +val;
        }
```

```
        set param2(val) {
                this._param2 = +val;
        }

        get param1() {
                return "This is param1: " + this._param1;
        }

        get sum() {
                return this._param1 + this._param2;
        }

        static description() {
                return "This is a static method, like the ones you're used
                to using...";
        }
}

let sampleObj = new SampleClass(1,2);
console.log(sampleObj.sum);

sampleObj.param1 = "100";
console.log(sampleObj.sum);
console.log(sampleObj.param1);
console.log(SampleClass.description());
```

Like I said, nothing controversial nor complicated, the code sample shows the basic features of the classes that come with ES6, which are:

- Inheritance: Using the extends reserved word, you can quickly tell which class inherits from another one.

- Reserved word constructor: Yes, you do have a quirk here; instead of following the old convention of using the class name to identify the constructor code, you can actually define it using a function called constructor.

- Getters and setters: This is one that I actually think is pretty neat. You get methods that you can define to add extra code needed when setting or getting a specific property on your class.

- No privacy in your code: There is no way to define the visibility of your methods and properties; everything is public, deal with it.

- Static methods: Finally, we also got static methods, which help to clean up the code.

Tip   Setters are quite useful and easy to set up; just remember to not name them exactly like the property you're trying to affect, otherwise you'll get a recursion error trying to setting inside the actual setter.

Functional Programming Support

JavaScript is not a functional programming language; but then again, it does have support for some of its features (see Listings 3-18, 3-19, and 3-20), such as having first-class citizen functions, allowing you to pass them around like parameters, and returning closures easily. This feature makes it possible to work with callbacks, which, as you've already seen, is the basis for asynchronous programming.

Let's look at a quick and simple functional programming example in Listing 3-19 (remember, JavaScript provides only some functional programming goodies, not all of them). Create an adder function.

Listing 3-19. Simple Example of an Adder Function Defined Using Functional Programming

```
function adder(x){
  return function(y) {
    return x+y
  }
}
var add10 = adder(10) //you create a new function that adds 10 to whatever
you pass to it.
console.log(add10(100)) //will output 110
```

Let's look at a more complex example, an implementation of the map function, which allows you to transform the values of an array by passing the array and the transformation function. Let's first look at how you'd use the *map* function.

Listing 3-20. Example of a Map Function Being Used

```
map([1,2,3,4], x => { return x * 2 }) //will return [2,4,6, 8]
map(["h","e","l","l","o"], String.prototype.toUpperCase)
//will return ["H","E","L","L","O"]
```

Now let's look at a possible implementation using the functional approach.

Listing 3-21. Implementation of a Map Function, Like the One Used in Listing 3-19

```
function reduce(list, fn, init) {
        if(list.length == 0) return init
        let value = list[0]
        init.push(fn.apply(value, [value])) //this will allow us to get
        both the functions that receive the value as parameters and the
        methods that use it from it's context (like toUpperCase)
        return reduce(list.slice(1), fn, init) //iterate over the list
        using it's tail (everything but the first element)
}
function map(list, fn) {
        return reduce(list, fn, [])
}
```

Duck Typing

Have you ever heard the phrase "If it looks like a duck, swims like a duck, and quacks like a duck, it probably is a duck"? Well then, it's the same for typing in JavaScript. The type of a variable is determined by its content and properties, not by a fixed value. So the same variable can change its type during the life cycle of your script. Duck typing is both a very powerful feature and a dangerous feature at the same time.

Listing 3-22 offers a simple demonstration.

Listing 3-22. Quick Example of Duck Typing in JavaScript

```
var foo = "bar"
console.log(typeof foo) //will output "string"
foo = 10
console.log(typeof foo) //this will now output "number"
```

Native Support for JSON

This is a tricky one, since JSON actually spawned from JavaScript, but let's not get into the whole chicken-and-egg thing here. Having *native* support for the main transport language used nowadays is a big plus.

Listing 3-23 is a simple example following the JSON syntax.

Listing 3-23. Example of How JSON Is Natively Supported by JavaScript

```
var myJSONProfile = {
        "first_name": "Fernando",
        "last_name": "Doglio",
        "current_age": 30,
        "married": true,
        "phone_numbers": [
                {
                        "home_phone": "59881000293",
                        "cell_phone": "59823142242"
                }
        ]
}

//And you can interact with that JSON without having to parse it or
anything
console.log(myJSONProfile.first_name, myJSONProfile.last_name)
```

This particular feature is especially useful in several cases—for instance, when working with a document-based storage solution (like MongoDB) because the modeling of data ends up being native in both places (your app and the database). Also, when developing an API, you've already seen that the transport language of choice these days is JSON, so the ability to format your responses directly with native notation (you could even just output your entities, for that matter) is a very big plus when it comes to ease of use.

The list could be extended, but those are some pretty powerful features that JavaScript and Node.js bring to the table without asking too much of the developer. They are quite easy to understand and use.

> **Note**   The features mentioned are not unique to JavaScript; other scripting languages have some of them as well.

npm: The Node Package Manager

Another point in favor of Node.js is its amazing package manager. As you might know by now (or are about to find out), development in Node is very module-dependent, meaning that you're not going to be developing the entire thing; most likely, you'll be reusing someone else's code in the form of modules.

This is a very important aspect of Node.js, because this approach allows you to focus on what makes your application unique and lets the generic code be integrated seamlessly. You don't have to recode the library for HTTP connectivity, nor your route handler on every project (in other words, you don't have to keep reinventing the wheel); just set the dependencies of your project into the package.json file using the best-suited module names, and then npm will take care of going through the whole dependency tree and will install everything needed (think of APT for Ubuntu or Homebrew for Mac).

The amount of active users and modules available (more than 100,000 packages and more than 600 million downloads a month) assures you that you'll find what you need; and in the rare occasions when you don't, you can contribute by uploading that specific module to the registry and help the next developer that comes looking for it.

This amount of modules can also be a bad thing since such a large number means that there will be several modules that try to do the same thing. (For instance, e-mail-validation, sane-e-mail-validation, mailcover, and mailgun-e-mail-validation all try to do the same thing—validate an e-mail address using different techniques; depending on your needs, you have to pick one.) You have to browse through them to find the best suited candidate.

This is all possible thanks to the amazing community of developers that have formed since Node.js hit the shelves in 2009.

To start using npm, just visit their site at `www.npmjs.org`. There you'll see a list of recently updated packages to get you started (as seen in Figure 3-5) and some of the most popular ones as well.

Figure 3-5. *The npm site*

If want to install it directly, just write the following line into your Linux console:

```
$ curl https://www.npmjs.org/install.sh | sh
```

You need to have Node.js version 0.8+ installed to use it properly. Once that is done, you can begin installing modules by simply typing:

```
$ npm install [MODULE_NAME]
```

This command downloads the specified module into a local folder called node_modules; so try to run it from within your project's folder.

You can also use npm to develop your own modules and publish them into the site by using the following:

```
$ npm publish #run this command from within your project's folder
```

The preceding command takes attributes from the package.json file, packages the module, and uploads everything into npm's registry. After that, you can go into the site and check for your package; it'll be listed there.

Note   Aside from checking out `www.npmjs.org`, you can also check the Google Groups nodejs[9] and nodejs-dev[10] for a direct connection to people in the Node.js community.

Who's Using Node.js?

This entire book is meant to validate and provide examples of how good Node.js is when it comes to developing RESTful systems, but also how valid the idea of having Node.js-powered systems running in production (this is the hardest obstacle to overcome, especially when trying to convince your boss of switching stacks into a Node.js-based one).

But what better validation, then, than to look at some of the most important users of Node.js in production?

- *PayPal*: Uses Node.js to power its web application

- *eBay*: Uses Node.js mainly due to the benefits that asynchronous I/O brings

- *LinkedIn*: The entire back-end mobile stack is done in Node.js. The two reasons for using it are scale and performance gained over the previous stack.

- *Netflix*: Uses Node.js on several services; often writes about experiences using Node.js on its tech blog at `http://techblog.netflix.com`

- *Yahoo!*: Uses Node.js on several products, such as Flickr, My Yahoo!, and home page)

This list could go on and include a very large list of other companies, some more well-known than others, but the point remains: Node.js is used for production services all over the Internet, and it handles all kinds of traffic.

---

[9]See `https://groups.google.com/forum/#!forum/nodejs`.
[10]See `https://groups.google.com/forum/#!forum/nodejs-dev`.

Summary

This chapter covered the advantages of Node.js for the common developer, especially how its features improve the performance of I/O–heavy systems such as APIs.

In the next chapter, you'll get more hands-on and learn about the basic architecture and tools you'll use to develop the API in the final chapter.

CHAPTER 4

Architecting a REST API

It is extremely important to understand a REST-based architecture, meaning how the system will look if you're basing all of your services in the REST style. But it is equally important to know what the internal architecture of those REST services will look like before you start working.

In Node.js there are several modules out there, with thousands of daily downloads that can help you create an API without having to worry too much about the internal aspects of it. And that might be a good idea if you're in a hurry to get the product out, but since you're here to learn, I'll go over all the components that make up a standard, general-purpose REST API.

The modules are mentioned, but I won't go into details on how they're used or anything; that will come in the next chapter—so keep reading!

For the purpose of this book, I'll take the traditional approach when it comes to architecting the API, and you'll use an MVC pattern (model–view–controller); although you might be familiar with other options, it is one of the most common ones and it normally fits well as a web use case.

The basic internal architecture of a RESTful API contains the following items:

- *A request handler*: This is the focal point that receives every request and processes it before doing anything else.

- *A middleware/pre-process chain*: These guys help shape the request and provide some help for authentication control.

- *A routes handler*: After the request handler is done, and the request itself has been checked and enriched with everything you need, this component figures out who needs to take care of the request.

- *The controller*: This guy is responsible for all requests done related to one specific resource.

© Fernando Doglio 2018
F. Doglio, *REST API Development with Node.js*, https://doi.org/10.1007/978-1-4842-3715-1_4

- *The Model*: Also known as the *resource* in our case. You'll focus most of the logic related to the resource in here.

- *The representation layer*: This layer takes care of creating the representation that is visible to the client app.

- *The response handler*: Last but certainly not least, the response handler takes care of sending the representation of the response back to the client.

Note   As I've stated several times before, this book focuses on HTTP-based REST, which means that any request mentioned in this chapter is an HTTP request, unless otherwise stated.

The Request Handler, the Pre-Process Chain, and the Routes Handler

The *request handler*, the *pre-process chain*, and the *routes handler* are the first three components in any request to your system, so they're key to having a responsive and fast API. Luckily, you're using Node.js, and as you saw in Chapter 3, Node.js is great at handling many concurrent requests because of its event loop and async I/O.

That being said, let's list the attributes our request handler needs to have for our RESTful system to work as expected:

- It has to gather all the HTTP headers and the body of the request, parse them, and provide a request object with that information.

- It needs to be able to communicate with both the pre-processing chain module and the routes handler to figure out which controller needs to be executed.

- It needs to create a response object capable of finishing and (optionally) writing a response back to the client.

Figure 4-1 shows the steps that are part of the initial contact between client and server:

1. The client application issues a request for a particular resource.

2. The request handler gathers all information. It creates a request object and passes it along to the pre-processing chain.

3. Once finished, the pre-processing chain returns the request object—with whatever changes made to it—to the request handler.

4. Finally, the RH sends the request and response objects to the routes handler so that the process can continue.

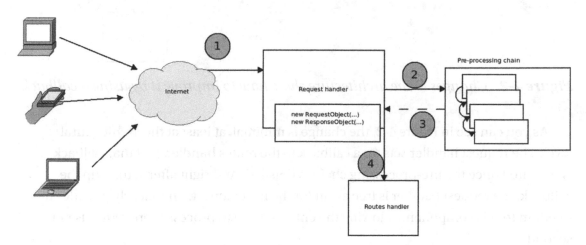

Figure 4-1. *Example of how the request handler and its interactions with other components look*

There is one problem in Figure 4-1 that jumps right out at you (or it should): if the pre-processing chain takes too long, the request handler must wait for it to finish before handing over the request to the routes handler, and any other incoming request is forced to wait as well.

This can be especially harmful to the performance of the API if the pre-processing chain is doing some heavy-duty tasks, like loading user-related data or querying external services.

Thanks to the fact that you're using Node.js as the basis for everything here, you can easily change the pre-processing chain to be an asynchronous operation. By doing that, the request handler is able to receive new requests while still waiting for the processing chain from the previous request. Figure 4-2 shows how the diagram would change.

Figure 4-2. *Changes to the architecture show how to improve it by using a callback*

As you can see in Figure 4-2, the change is minimal, at least at the architectural level. The request handler sets up a callback to the routes handler, and that callback is executed once the pre-processing chain is finished. And right after setting up the callback, the request handler is free again for the next request. This clearly provides more freedom to this component, allowing the entire system to process more requests per second.

Note   This change will not actually speed up the pre-processing chain time of execution. Neither will it speed up the time it takes a single request to be finished, but it will allow the API to handle more requests per second, which in practice means avoiding an obvious bottleneck.

As for the pre-processing chain, you'll use it for generic operations, things that are required in most of the routes you'll handle. That way you can extract that code from the handlers and centralize it into small units of code (functions) that are called in sequence for every request.

Most of the modules you'll see in Chapter 5 have one version of the pre-processing chain. For instance, Express.js calls the functions that can be executed in the chain "middleware." Vatican.js calls them "pre-processors" to differentiate them from the post-processors that the module also provides.

Tip   The main rule to remember when adding a new function into this chain is that as a good practice, the function should take care of one task, and one task only. (This is generally a good practice to follow on every aspect of software development. Some call it the Unix Philosophy, others call it KISS; call it whatever you want, it's a good idea to keep in mind.) That way, it becomes mind-blowingly easy to enable and disable them when testing, even to alter their order. On the other hand, if you start adding functions that take care of more than one thing, like authenticating the user and loading his/her preferences, you'll have to edit the function's code to disable one of those services.

Since you'll want the entire pre-processing to be done asynchronously to release the request handler from waiting for the chain to be done, the chain will use asynchronous serial flow. This way you can be sure of the order of execution; but at the same time, you're free to have these functions perform actions that take longer than normal, like asynchronous calls to external services, I/O operations, and the like.

Let's take a final look at the last diagram. So far it looks great: you're able to handle requests asynchronously and you can do some interesting things to the request by pre-processing it before giving it to the routes handler. But there is one catch: the pre-processing chain is the same for all routes.

That might not be a problem if the API is small enough, but just to be on the safe side, and to provide a fully scalable architecture, let's take a look at another change that can be done over the current version to provide the freedom you require (see Figure 4-3).

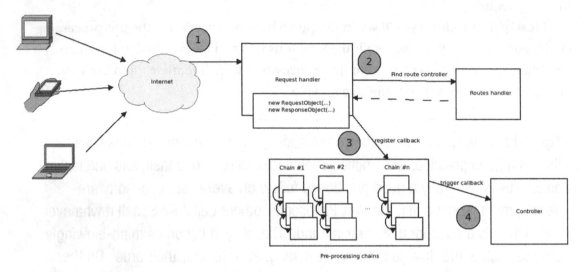

Figure 4-3. *Change on the architecture to provide room for multiple pre-processing chains*

This chain (as shown in Figure 4-3) is bigger than the previous one, but it does solve the scaling problem. The process has now changed into the following steps:

1. The client application issues a request for a particular resource.

2. The request handler gathers all information. It creates a request object and passes it along to the request handler to return the right controller. This action is simple enough to do synchronously. Ideally, it should be done in constant time (O(1)).

3. Once it has the controller, it registers an asynchronous operation with the correct pre-processing chain. This time around, the developer is able to set up as many chains as needed and associates them to one specific route. The request handler also sets up the controller's method to be executed as the callback to the chain's process.

4. Finally, the callback is triggered, and the request and response objects are passed into the controller's method to continue the execution.

Note   Step 2 mentions that the controller lookup based on the request should be done in constant time. This is not a hard requirement but should be the desirable result; otherwise, when handling many concurrent requests, this step might become a bottleneck that can affect subsequent requests.

MVC: a.k.a. Model–View–Controller

The model–view–controller (MVC) architectural pattern[1] is probably *the most well-known pattern out there*. Forget about the Gang of Four's design patterns,[2] forget about everything you learned about software design and architectural patterns; if you're comfortable with MVC, then you have nothing to worry about.

Actually, that's not true; well, most of it isn't anyway. MVC *is* currently among the most well-known and used design patterns on web projects (that much is true). That being said, you should not forget about the others; in fact, I highly recommend you actually get familiar with the most common design patterns (aside from MVC of course), like Singleton, Factory, Builder, Adapter, Composite, Decorator, and so forth. Just look them up, and read and study some examples; it's always handy to have them as part of your tool box.

Going back to MVC, even though it has become really popular in the last few years, especially since 2007 (coincidently the year when version 2 of Ruby on Rails, a popular web framework that had MVC as part of its core architecture, was released), this bad boy is not new. In fact, it was originally described by Krasner and Pope in 1988 at SmallTalk-80[3] as a design pattern for creating user interfaces.

The reason why it is such a popular pattern on web projects is because it fits perfectly into the multilayer architecture that the web provides. Think about it: due to the client–server architecture, you already have two layers there, and if you organized code to split some responsibilities between orchestration and business logic, you gain one more layer on the server side, which could translate into the scenario shown in Table 4-1.

---

[1]See http://en.wikipedia.org/wiki/Model%E2%80%93view%E2%80%93controller.

[2]See http://www.amazon.com/Design-Patterns-Elements-Reusable-Object-Oriented/dp/0201633612/.

[3]See http://dl.acm.org/citation.cfm?id=50757.50759.

Table 4-1. *List of Layers*

Layer	Description
Business logic	You can encapsulate the business logic of the system into different components, which you can call *models*. They represent the different resources that the system handles.
Orchestration	The models know how to do their job, but not when or what kind of data to use. The controllers take care of this.
Representation layer	Handles creating the visual representation of the information. In a normal web application, this is the HTML page. In a RESTful API, this layer takes care of the different representations each resource has.

Note   Prior to Table 4-1, I mentioned that the client–server architecture provided the first two layers for MVC, meaning that the client would act as the presentation layer. This is not entirely true, as you see later on, but it does serve as a conceptual layer, meaning that you'll need a way for the application to present the information to the user (client).

Let's look at the diagram in Figure 4-4, which represents Table 4-1.

Figure 4-4. *The interaction between the three layers*

Figure 4-4 shows the decoupling of the three components: the controller, the model (which in this case you can also call the resource), and the view. This decoupling allows for a clear definition of each component's responsibilities, which in turn helps keep the code clean and easy to understand.

Although this is great, the pattern has changed a bit ever since it was adopted by some web development frameworks, like Ruby on Rails; it now looks more like what's shown in Figure 4-5.

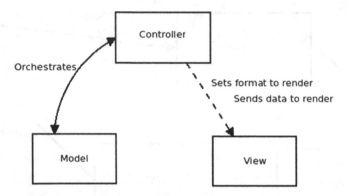

Figure 4-5. *MVC applied to the web*

The current iteration of the pattern removed the relationship between the model and the view, and instead gave the controller that responsibility. The controller now also orchestrates the view.

This final version is the one you'll add into our current growing architecture. Let's take a look at how it will look (see Figure 4-6).

Figure 4-6. *The architecture with the added MVC pattern*

Steps 5 and 6 have been added to our architecture. When the right method on the controller is triggered (in step 4), it handles interacting with the model, gathers the required data, and then sends it over to the view to render it back to the client application.

This architecture works great, but there is still one improvement that can be done. With our RESTful API, the representations are strictly related to the resources data structure, and you can generalize the view into a view layer, which will take care of transforming the resources into whatever format you require. This change simplifies the development since you centralize the entire view-related code into one single component (the view layer).

The diagram in Figure 4-7 might not have changed a lot, but the change in the view box into a view layer represents the generalization of that code, which initially implied that there would be one specific view code for every resource.

Figure 4-7. *View layer added to the architecture*

Alternatives to MVC

MVC is a great architecture. Nearly every developer is using it or has used it for a web project. Of course, not everyone loves it, because it has suffered the same fate other popular things in the development community have suffered (Ruby on Rails, anyone?). If it becomes popular on the Internet, everyone is using it for everything—until they realize that not every project looks like an MVC nail, so you have to start looking at other shapes of hammers (other alternatives architectures).

But luckily, there are alternatives; there are similar architectural patterns that may better suit your needs, depending on the particular aspects of your project. Some of them are direct derivatives of MVC, and others try to approach the same problem from a slightly different angle (I say "slightly" because, as you're about to see, there are things in common).

Hierarchical MVC

Hierarchical MVC[4] is a more complex version of MVC in the sense that you can nest one MVC component inside another one. This gives developers the ability to have things like an MVC group for a page, another MVC group for the navigation inside the page, and a final MVC component for the contents of the page.

This approach is especially helpful when developing reusable widgets that can be plugged into components, since each MVC group is self-contained. It is useful in cases when the data to be displayed come from different related sources. In these cases, having an HMVC structure helps keep the separation of concerns intact and avoids coupling between components that shouldn't be.

Let's look at a very basic example. Think of a user reading a blog post and the related comments underneath it. There are two ways to go about it: with MVC or with HMVC.

With MVC, the request is done to the BlogPosts controller, since that is the main resource being requested; afterward, that controller loads the proper blog post model, and using that model's ID, it loads the related comments models. Right there, there is an unwanted coupling between the BlogPosts controller and the comments model. You can see this in the diagram in Figure 4-8.

---

[4]See http://en.wikipedia.org/wiki/Hierarchical_model%E2%80%93view%E2%80%93controller.

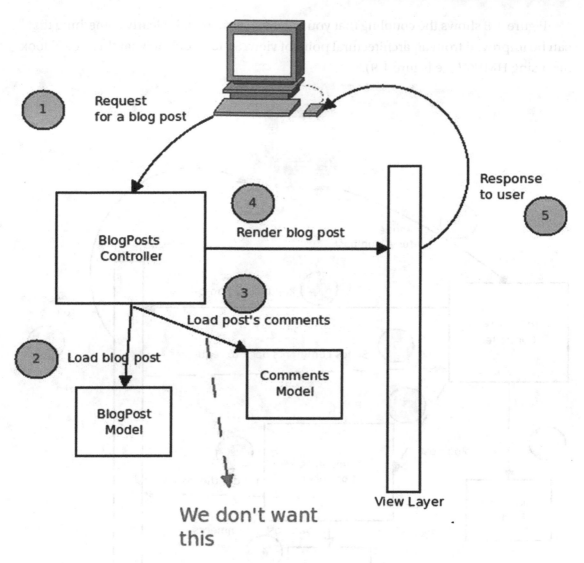

Figure 4-8. *The problem that HMVC tries to solve*

Figure 4-8 shows the coupling that you need to get rid of; it is clearly something that can be improved from an architectural point of view. So let's look at what this would look like using HMVC (see Figure 4-9).

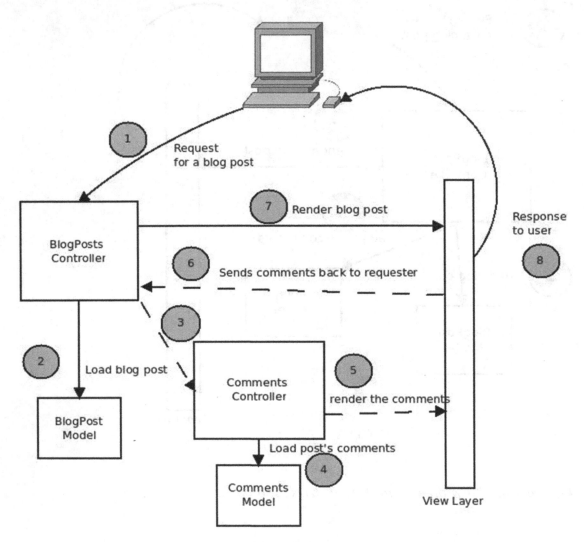

Figure 4-9. *The same diagram with the HMVC pattern applied*

The architecture certainly looks more complex and there are more steps, but it is also cleaner and easier to extend. Now in step 3, you're sending a request to an entirely new MVC component, one in charge of dealing with comments. That component will in turn interact with the corresponding model and with the generic view layer to return the representation of the comments. The representation is received by the BlogPost controller, which attaches it to the data obtained from the BlogPost model and sends everything back into the view layer.

If you want to create a new section in the blog showing specific blog posts and their comments, you could easily reuse the comments component.

All in all, this pattern could be considered a specialization of common MVC, and it could come in handy when designing complex systems.

Model–View–ViewModel

The Model–View–ViewModel pattern[5] was created by Microsoft in 2005 as a way to facilitate UI development using WPF and Silverlight; it allows UI developers to write code using a markup language (called XAML) focusing on the User Experience (UX), and accessing the dynamic functionalities using bindings to the code. This approach allows developers and UX developers to work independently without affecting each other's work.

Just like with MVC, the Model in this architecture concentrates the business logic, while the ViewModel acts as a mediator between the Model and the View, exposing the data from the Model. It also contains most of the view logic, allowing the ViewLayer to only focus on displaying information, leaving all dynamic behavior to the ViewModel (see Figure 4-10 for more details).

Figure 4-10. *An MVVC architecture*

These days, the pattern has been adopted by others outside Microsoft, like the ZK framework in Java and KnockoutJS, AngularJS, Vue.js, and other frameworks in JavaScript (since MVVM is a pattern specializing in UI development, it makes sense that UI frameworks written in JavaScript are big adopters of this pattern).

---

[5]See http://en.wikipedia.org/wiki/Model_View_ViewModel.

Model–View–Adapter

The model–view–adapter[6] (MVA) pattern is very similar to MVC, but with a couple of differences. Mainly, in MVC the main business logic is concentrated inside each model, which also contains the main data structure, with the controller in charge of orchestrating the model and the view.

In MVA, the model is just the data that you're working with, and the business logic is concentrated in the adapter, which is in charge of interacting both with the view and the model. So basically, it consists of slimmer models and fatter controllers. But joking aside, this allows for a total decoupling of the view and the model, giving all responsibilities to the adapter.

This approach works great when switching adapters to achieve different behaviors on the same view and model.

The architecture for this pattern is shown in Figure 4-11.

Figure 4-11.   *The MVA pattern shown as a diagram*

Response Handler

The final component to our API architecture is the *response handler*; it is in charge of grabbing the resource representation from the view layer and sending it back to the client. The response format (which is not the same as the representation's format) must be the same as the request's format; in this case, it'll be an HTTP 1.1 message.

The HTTP response has two parts: the header, which contains several fields specifying properties about the message, and the body. The content of the message's body is the actual representation of the resource. The header is the section that interests us the most right now; it contains fields like content-type, content-length, and so on.

---

[6]See http://en.wikipedia.org/wiki/Model%E2%80%93view%E2%80%93adapter.

Some of those fields are mandatory and some of them are required if you intend to follow the REST style fully (which you do).

- *Cacheable*: From the constraints imposed by REST defined in Chapter 1. Every request must be explicitly or implicitly set as cacheable when applicable. This translates into the use of the HTTP header `cache-control`.

- *Content-type:* The content type of the response's body is important for the client application to understand how to parse the data. If your resources only have one possible representation, the content type might be an optional header since you could notify the client app developer about the format through your documentation. But if you were to change it in the future, or add a new one, then it might cause some serious damage to your clients. So consider this header mandatory.

- *Status*: The status code is not mandatory but extremely important, as I've mentioned in previous chapters. It provides the client application a quick indicator of the result of the request.

- *Date:* This field should contain the date and time when the message was sent. It should be in HTTP-date format[7] (e.g., Fri, 24 Dec 2014 23:34:45 GMT).

- *Content-length:* This field should contain the number of bytes (length) of the body of the message transferred.

Let's look at an example of an HTTP response with the JSON representation of a resource:

```
HTTP/1.0 200 OK
Date: Fri, 31 Dec 1999 23:59:59 GMT
Content-Type: application/json
Cache-control: private, max-age=0, no-cache
Content-Length: 1354

{
```

---

[7]See `http://tools.ietf.org/html/rfc7231#section-7.1.1.1`.

```
    "name": "J.K.Rolling",
    "id": "ab12351bac",
    "books": [
        {
            "title": "Harry Potter and the Philosopher's Stone",
            "isbn": "9788478888566"
        },
      {
          "title": "Harry Potter and the Prisoner of Azkaban",
          "isbn": "9788422685227"
      }
    ]
}
```

There is one more improvement that could be made on the response handler if you want to get some extra juice. This is entirely extra, and most of the Node.js frameworks out there don't have it (with the exception of Vatican.js).

The idea is to have a post-processing chain of functions that receives the response content returned by the view layer, and transforms it, or enriches it if you will, with further data. It would act as the first version of the pre-processing chain: one common chain for the entire process.

With this idea, you can abstract further code from the controllers just by moving it into the post-processing stage. Code-like schema validation (which I'll discuss later in the book) or response header setup can be centralized here, and with the added extra of a simple mechanism for switching your code around or disabling steps in the chain.

Let's take a look at the final architecture of our API (see Figure 4-12).

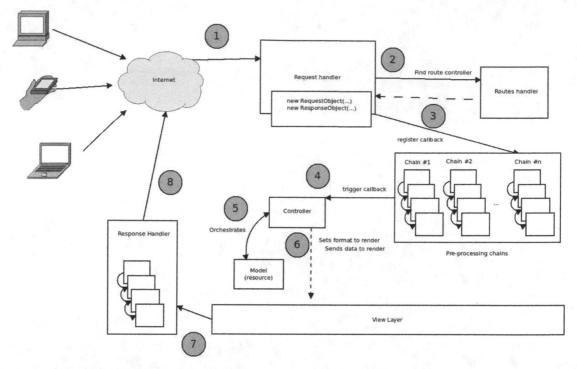

Figure 4-12. *The final architecture with the response handler and the added post-processing chain*

Summary

This chapter covered the basics for a complete and functional RESTful API architecture. It even covered some extras that aren't required but are certainly nice to have, such as pre-and post-processing. You also looked at the main architecture behind our design (MVC) and some alternatives to it, in case your requirements aren't a perfect match for the MVC model.

In the next chapter, I'll start talking about the modules you'll use to write the implementation of this architecture.

CHAPTER 5

Working with Modules

As I discussed in Chapter 3, Node.js has a huge community of developers behind it; they are willing to put hours and effort into providing the rest of the people in that community with high-quality modules.

In this chapter, I'll talk about some of those modules; you'll see how to use them to get the architecture described in Chapter 4.

More specifically, you'll need modules for the following parts:

- *HTTP request and response handling*: This is the most basic feature. As you're about to see, there are plenty of options out there to pick from.

- *Routes handling*: Aside from the preceding, request handling is one of the most important and crucial parts of our system.

- *Pre-processing chain (middleware)*: You can leave out post-processing because it's a less common feature, but pre-processing (or middleware) is common and very useful.

- *Up-to-date documentation*: This wasn't part of our architecture, but I did mention it in Chapter 2, when I talked about good practices. And it so happens that there is a module that will help here, so you might as well add it.

- *Hypermedia on the response*: Again, not part of the architecture, but part of a REST, so you'll add it using the HAL standard.

- *Response and request format validation*: Finally, this will be an added bonus; as a good practice, always validate the format of the requests and responses.

© Fernando Doglio 2018
F. Doglio, *REST API Development with Node.js*, https://doi.org/10.1007/978-1-4842-3715-1_5

Our Alternatives

Instead of looking at each point individually, you'll take a look at each of the modules, and I'll evaluate them accordingly. Some of them, as you'll see, handle more than just one thing, which sometimes comes in handy because getting unrelated modules to work together is not always an easy task.

Request/Response Handling

Regarding request and response handling, they usually both come in the same module. They are the basics of every HTTP application you intend to make. If you don't know how to handle the HTTP protocol, you can't move forward.

And because Node.js is such a good fit for HTTP applications, there are quite a few modules that will help you in this task. You need something that can do the following:

- Listen on a specific port for HTTP traffic

- Translate the HTTP message into a JavaScript object so that you can read it and use it without having to worry about parsing it or about any of the details of the HTTP protocol

- Write an HTTP response without having to worry about the HTTP message format

Writing code that listens in a specific port for HTTP traffic is simple; actually, Node.js provides all the tools you need, out of the box, to achieve the three preceding points. Then why do we need extra modules if we can easily do it ourselves? That's a very valid question, and to be honest, it all depends on your needs. If the system you're building is small enough, then it might be a good idea to build the HTTP server yourself; otherwise, it's always good to use a well-tested and tried module. These modules also solve other related issues for you, such as routes handling, so going with a third-party module might be a good choice.

Routes Handling

Routes handling is tightly coupled with request and response handling; it's the next step in the processing of the request. Once you translate the HTTP message into an actual JavaScript object that you can work with, you need to know which piece of code needs to handle it. This is where routes handling comes in.

There are two sides to this part. First, you need to be able to set up the routes in your code and associate the handler's code with one or more specific routes. And then the system needs to grab the route of the requested resource and match it to one of yours. That might not be such an easy task. Remember that most routes in any complex system have parameterized parts for things like unique IDs and other parameters. For example, take a look at Table 5-1.

Table 5-1. *Routing Example*

This...	.... Needs to Match This
/v1/books/1234412	/v1/books/:id
/v1/authors/jkrowling/books	/v1/:author_name/books

Usually, routing frameworks provide some sort of templating language that allows developers to set up named parameters in the route template. Later the framework will match the requested URLs to the templates, taking into consideration those variable parts added. Different frameworks add different variations of this; you'll see some of them in a bit.

Middleware

This is the name that the pre-processing chain normally gets in the Node.js world, and that is because the Connect[1] framework (which is the framework on which most other web frameworks are based) has this functionality.

I already talked about this topic in the previous chapter, so let's look at some examples (Listing 5-1) of middleware functions that are compatible with Connect-based frameworks:

---

[1]See https://www.npmjs.com/package/connect.

Listing 5-1. Examples of Middleware Functions

```
//Logs every request into the standard output
function logRequests(req, res, next) {
    console.log("[", req.method, "]", req.url)
    next()
}

/*
Makes sure that the body of the request is a valid json object, otherwise,
it throws an error
*/
function formatRequestBody(req, res, next)  {
    if(typeof req.body == 'string') {
      try {
        req.body = JSON.parse(req.body)
      } catch (ex) {
        next("invalid data format")
      }
    }
    next()
}
```

The two examples from Listing 5-1 are different, but at the same time they share a common function signature. Every middleware function receives three parameters: the request object, the response object, and the next function. The most interesting bit here is the last parameter, the next function, calling it is mandatory unless you want to end the processing chain right there. It calls the next middleware in the chain, unless you pass in a value, in which case it'll call the first error handler it finds and it'll pass it the parameter (normally an error message or object).

The use of middleware is very common for things like authentication, logging, session handling, and so forth.

Up-to-Date Documentation

As I've already discussed, keeping up-to-date documentation of the API's interface is crucial if you want developers to use your system. I'll go over some modules that will help in that area. There is no silver bullet, of course; some of modules add more overhead than others, but the main goal is to have some sort of system that updates its documentation as automatically as possible.

Hypermedia on the Response

If you want to follow the REST style to the letter, you need to work this into your system. It is one of the most forgotten features of REST—and a great one, since it allows for self-discovery, another characteristic of a RESTful system.

For this particular case, you'll go with a pre-defined standard called HAL (covered in Chapter 1), so you'll be checking out some modules that allow you to work with this particular format.

Response and Request Validation

I'll also go over some modules that will let you validate both the response and the request format. Our API will work with JSON alone, but it's always useful to validate the structure of that JSON in the request due to errors in the client application and in the response to ensure that there are no errors in the server side after code changes.

Adding a validation on every request might be too big of an overhead, so an alternative might be a test suite that takes care of doing the validation when executed. But the request format validation will have to be done on every request to ensure that the execution of your system is not tainted by an invalid request.

The List of Modules

Now let's go over some modules that take care of one or several of the categories mentioned; for each one, you'll list the following attributes:

- The name of the module

- The category it fits into

- The currently released version

- A small description
- The home page URL
- The installation instructions
- Code examples

We won't compare them because it's not an easy thing to do considering that some modules only handle one thing, whereas others take care of several things. So after going over them, I'll propose a combination of these modules, but you will have enough information to pick a different combo if it better fits your problem.

HAPI

HAPI is a framework used for building both applications and services (APIs). It's actively maintained and has more than half a million downloads a month.

Table 5-2 shows more details about this particular framework.

Table 5-2. *HAPI Module Information*

Category	Request/Response handler, Routes handler
Current version	17.4.0
Description	HAPI is a configuration-centric web framework designed to create any kind of web application, including APIs. The main goal of HAPI is to allow developers to focus on coding the logic of an application, leaving infrastructure code to the framework.
Home page URL	`http://hapijs.com/`

Installation	Installing the framework is simple using npm:
	$ npm install hapi
	That's it. HAPI is installed in your application. You can also run the following command to get the dependency added automatically to your `package.json` file:
	$ npm install hapi --save

Code Examples

After installation, the most basic thing you can do to initialize the system and get your server up and running is shown in Listing 5-2.

Listing 5-2. Simple Server Code with HAPI.JS

```
'use strict';
const Hapi=require('hapi');
// Create a server with a host and port
const server=Hapi.server({
    host:'localhost',
    port:8000
});
// Start the server
async function start() {
    try {
        await server.start();
    }
    catch (err) {
        console.log(err);
        process.exit(1);
    }
    console.log('Server running at:', server.info.uri);
}
start()
```

As you can see, this example is quite basic, but the steps required to initialize the application are there. The `server.start` line initializes a server object with the new connection selected. That means you could maintain several open connections at the same time, as shown in Listing 5-3.

After executing the code from Listing 5-2, you get the following line:

```
Server running at: http://localhost:8000
```

And if you try to browse to `http://localhost:8000`, all you'll get is the response from Figure 5-1, which is absolutely normal, because even though you've created a web server, you haven't registered any routes yet.

127

```
{
    statusCode: 404,
    error: "Not Found",
    message: "Not Found"
}
```

Figure 5-1. *404 error from HAPI.JS*

Listing 5-3. Example of Two Different Servers Being Started on Different Ports

```
'use strict';
const Hapi=require('hapi');
// Create a server with a host and port
const server=Hapi.server({
    host:'localhost',
    port:8000
});

const adminServer = Hapi.server({
        host: 'localhost',
        port: 8001
});

// Add a route to list users
adminServer.route({
    method:'GET',
    path:'/users',
    handler:function(request,h) {
        //your code here
    }
});
```

```
// Start the server
async function start() {
    try {
        await server.start();
        await adminServer.start();
    }
    catch (err) {
        console.log(err);
        process.exit(1);
    }
    console.log('Servers running at: ', server.info.uri, ' and ',
    adminServer.info.uri);
}
start()
```

This code initializes the application, which in turn sets up two different servers: one for the API itself and another one for an admin system. In this code you can also see how easy it is to set up routes with HAPI. Although the code can clearly be cleaned up and the routes definitions can be taken out to a separate file, this is a great example of how two (or more!) servers with their respective routes can be configured using this framework.

Another interesting bit that HAPI provides is the route templates you can use by setting up your own. With it, you can use named parameters as seen in Listing 5-4.

Listing 5-4. Setting Up Routes with URL Templating in HAPI.JS

```
'use strict'
const Hapi = require('hapi');
const server = new Hapi.Server({
        host: 'localhost',
        port: 3000
});

const getAuthor = (request, reply) => {
    // here the author and book parameters are inside
    // request.params
};
```

```
server.route({
    path: '/{author}/{book?}',
    method: 'GET',
    handler: getAuthor
});
```

In the code from Listing 5-4, when setting up the route, anything that's inside curly brackets is considered a named parameter. The last parameter though, has a ? added to it, which means it's optional.

Note   Only the last named parameter can be set as optional; otherwise, it makes no sense.

In addition to the ?, you can use another special character to tell HAPI the number of segments a named parameter should match; that character is the * and it should be followed by a number greater than 1, or nothing, if you want it to match any number of segments.

Note   Just like the ? character, only the last parameter can be configured to match any number of segments.

Listing 5-5 shows some examples.

Listing 5-5. Multid-Segment Parameters Example

```
server.route({
    path: '/person/{name*2}',    // Matches '/person/john/doe'
    method: 'GET',
    handler: getPerson
});

server.route({
    path: '/author/{name*}',    // Matches '/author/j/k/rowling' or
    '/author/frank/herbert' or /author/
    method: 'GET',
    handler: getAuthor
});
```

130

```
function getAuthor(req, reply) {
   // The different segments can be obtained like this:
   let segments = req.params.name.split('/')
   //the rest of your code goes here...
}

function getPerson(req, reply) {
   let segments = req.params.name.split(''/')
   //the rest of your code here...
}
```

Express.js

This is one of the most common and used frameworks for Node. As you're about to see, it provides all the required building blocks for creating both web apps, and microservices. Table 5-3 shows more details about this framework.

Table 5-3. Express.js Module Information

Category	Request/Response handler, Routes handler, Middleware
Current version	4.16.3
Description	Express is a full-fledged web framework providing small and robust tools for HTTP servers, making it a great candidate for all kinds of web applications, including RESTful APIs.
Home page URL	`http://expressjs.com`
Installation	`$ npm install express`

Code Examples

Express.js is sometimes considered the de facto solution when it comes to building a web application in Node.js, much like Ruby on Rails was for Ruby for a long time.

That being said, it doesn't mean Express.js should be the only choice or that it is right choice for every project; so make sure that you are well-informed before choosing a web framework for your project.

This particular framework has evolved over the years, and now in version 4 it provides a generator. To initialize the entire project, you first have to install it with the following line:

```
$ npm install express-generator -g
```

After the installation is complete, you can use the following line:

```
$ express ./express-test
```

This line will generate an output like the one shown in Figure 5-2.

```
create : ./express-test
create : ./express-test/package.json
create : ./express-test/app.js
create : ./express-test/public
create : ./express-test/public/javascripts
create : ./express-test/public/images
create : ./express-test/routes
create : ./express-test/routes/index.js
create : ./express-test/routes/users.js
create : ./express-test/public/stylesheets
create : ./express-test/public/stylesheets/style.css
create : ./express-test/views
create : ./express-test/views/index.jade
create : ./express-test/views/layout.jade
create : ./express-test/views/error.jade
create : ./express-test/bin
create : ./express-test/bin/www

install dependencies:
  $ cd ./express-test && npm install

run the app:
  $ DEBUG=express-test:* ./bin/www
```

Figure 5-2. *Output of the express generator command*

The framework generates a lot of folders and files, but in general, it's the structure for a generic web application, one that has views, styles, JavaScript files, and other web app–related resources. This is not for us since we're building a RESTful API. You'll want to remove those folders (views and public, more specifically).

To finalize the process, just enter the folder and install the dependencies; this will leave you with a working web application. Check Listing 5-6 if you're curious about what it takes to initialize the framework (this is all created by Express as part of the init command).

Listing 5-6. Content of the app.js File Generated by Express

```
var express = require('express');
var path = require('path');
var favicon = require('serve-favicon');
var logger = require('morgan');
var cookieParser = require('cookie-parser');
var bodyParser = require('body-parser');

var index = require('./routes/index');
var users = require('./routes/users');

var app = express();

// view engine setup
app.set('views', path.join(__dirname, 'views'));
app.set('view engine', 'jade');

// uncomment after placing your favicon in /public
//app.use(favicon(path.join(__dirname, 'public', 'favicon.ico')));
app.use(logger('dev'));
app.use(bodyParser.json());
app.use(bodyParser.urlencoded({ extended: false }));
app.use(cookieParser());
app.use(express.static(path.join(__dirname, 'public')));

app.use('/', index);
app.use('/users', users);
```

```
// catch 404 and forward to error handler
app.use(function(req, res, next) {
  var err = new Error('Not Found');
  err.status = 404;
  next(err);
});

// error handler
app.use(function(err, req, res, next) {
  // set locals, only providing error in development
  res.locals.message = err.message;
  res.locals.error = req.app.get('env') === 'development' ? err : {};

  // render the error page
  res.status(err.status || 500);
      res.render('error');
});

module.exports = app;
```

Let's now take a look at Listing 5-7 and what it takes to set up a route in Express.js.

Listing 5-7. All That's Needed Is Just a Few Lines of Code

```
const express = require("express");
const app = express()
//...
app.get('/', (req, res)  => {
  console.log("Hello world!")
})
```

That's it. All that you need to remember when setting up a route is the following: **app.VERB(URL-TEMPLATE, HANDLER-FUNCTION)**. The handler function will receive three parameters: the request object, the response object, and the next function. The last parameter is only useful when you set up more than one handler for the same route and method combination; that way you can chain the methods like they are middleware.

Take a look at the following example in Listing 5-8:

Listing 5-8. Chaining Verbs to the Same URI

```
app.route('/users/:id')
   .all(checkAuthentication)
   .all(loadUSerData)
   .get(returnDataHandler)
   .put(updateUserHandler)
```

In the preceding code, there are several interesting things happening:

- A named parameter is used for the ID of the user.

- Two middleware functions are set up for every verb hitting the
  '/users/:id' route.

- It's setting up a handler for the GET method hitting the URL, and at
  the same time, it's setting up a handler for when the verb is PUT—all
  in the same line of code.

Express provides its own flavor of named parameters (you saw an example of that in the preceding code), but there are other things you can do. For instance, you can use regular expressions.

The code from Listing 5-9 matches both '/commit/5bc2ab' and '/commit/5bc2ab..57ba31', and you can see that getting the parameter inside the handler's code is simple too.

You can also set a callback function to do some processing when a specific named parameter is received (as seen in Listing 5-10); for instance:

Listing 5-9. Example Showing the Use of Regular Expressions to Define a Route

```
router.get(/^\/commit\/(\w+)(?:\.\.(\w+))?$/, (req, res) => {
  let from = req.params[0];
  let  to = req.params[1] || 'HEAD';
  res.send('commit range ' + from + '..' + to);
});
```

Listing 5-10. Cleaner Code Using Parameter-Specific Callbacks

```
const router = express.Router()
const express = require('express')
const app = express()

router.param('user_id', (req, res, next, id) => {
    loadUser(id, function(err, usr) {
        if(err) {
            next(new Error("There was an error loading the user's
            information")) //this will call erorr handler
        } else {
            req.user = usr
            next()
        }
    })

})
//then on the route definition

app.get('/users/:user_id', (req, res) => {
    //req.user is already defined and can be used
})
```

If there is an error on the user_id callback function, then the route's handler will never be called, because the first error handler will be called instead.

Finally, let's look at some examples of middleware usage inside Express.js. I already covered the basics for this type of function earlier, but you never saw how to use it with Express.js.

You can do it in two ways: set up a global middleware (Listing 5-11) or a route-specific middleware (Listing 5-12).

For a global middleware, you just do this:

Listing 5-11. Middleware Example

```
app.use((req, res, next) => {
    //your code here will be executed on every request
    next() //remember to call next unless you want the chain to end here.
})
```

For a route-specific middleware, you do this:

Listing 5-12. Route-Specific Middleware Syntax

```
app.use('/books', (req, res, next) => {
        //this function will only be called on this path
        next() //always important to call next unless you don't want the
        process' flow to continue.
})
```

You can even set up a route-specific stack of middleware, as seen in Listing 5-13.

Listing 5-13. Example of a Stack of Middleware for a Specific Store

```
app.use('/books', function(req, res, next){
    //this function will only be called on this path
    next() //always important to call next unless you don't want the
    process' flow to continue.
}, function(req, res, next) {
    //as long as you keep calling next, the framework will keep advancing
    in the chain until reaching the actual handler
      next()
})
```

Restify

You can think of Restify as a version of ExpressJS tailored to only be able to create RESTful APIs. Table 5-4 shows more details about this framework.

Table 5-4. *Restify Module's Information*

Category	Request/Response handler, Routes handler, Middleware
Current version	6.3.4
Description	Restify is a framework specifically designed for building REST APIs. It borrows heavily from Express.js (specifically, versions prior to 4.0) because Express is considered the standard when it comes to building web apps.
Home page URL	`http://restify.com/`
Installation	`$ npm install restify`

Code Examples

Restify borrows a lot of its features from Express, so I'll focus on the things that it adds; for other examples, please refer to the previous module or visit the Restify home page.

Initialization is simpler than with Express, although there are no code generators. The following code is all you need to start up a server:

Listing 5-14. Simple Web Server Creation with Restify

```
const restify = require('restify');

let server = restify.createServer({
    name: 'MyApp',
});

server.listen(8080);
```

The `createServer` method provides some helpful options that will simplify your job in the future. Table 5-5 lists some of Restify's options.

Table 5-5. *List of Restify Options*

Option	Description
certificate	For building HTTPS servers, pass in the path to the certificate here.
key	For building HTTPS servers, pass in the path to the key file here.
log	Optionally, you can pass in an instance of a logger. It needs to be an instance of node-bunyan.[2]
name	The name of the API. Used to set the server response header; by default it is "restify."
version	A default version for all routes.
formatters	A group of content formatters used for content-negotiation

In the most basic ways, routes are handled just like Express: you can either pass in the path template and the route handler, or you can pass in a regular expression and the handler.

In a more advanced way, Restify provides some goodies that Express doesn't. The following subsections provide some examples.

Naming Routes

You can set up names for specific routes, which will in turn allow you to jump from one handler to others using that attribute. Let's look at how to set up the names first.

Listing 5-15. Sample Code Showing How to Set Up Named Routes

```
server.get('/foo/:id',  (req, res, next) =>
  next('foo2')
);

server.get({
    name: 'foo2',
```

---

[2]See https://github.com/trentm/node-bunyan.

```
    path: '/foo/:id'
},  (req, res, next) => {
    res.send(200);
    next();
});
```

This code is setting up two different handlers for the same path, but Restify will only execute the first handler it finds, so the second one will never get executed unless the next statement is called with the name of the second route.

Naming is also used to reference routes when rendering the response, which allows for an interesting feature: hypermedia on the response. To be honest, the solution proposed by Restify is a bit basic and it doesn't really provide a good mechanism for automatically adding hypermedia for self-discovery, but it is more than most other frameworks do. Listing 5-16 shows an example of how it works.

Listing 5-16. Hypermedia on the Response Basic Example

```
const restify = require("restify")

let server = restify.createServer()

server.get({
    name: 'country-cities',
    path: '/country/:id/cities'
}, (req, res, next) => {
        res.send('cities') //no need to call the next function, we don't want
        to add anything after this step
})

server.get('/country/:id', function(req, res, next) {
  res.send({
    name: "Uruguay",
    cities: server.router.render('country-cities', {id: "uruguay"})
    })
})

server.listen(3000)
```

The example is quite basic, but it provides the required logic to understand that there is no need to know the URL structure needed to get a list of cities for a specific country from within the /countries/:id endpoint, which in turn provides easier maintenance if, in the future, that first URL needs to be changed.

Versioning Routes

Restify provides support for a global version number, as you saw earlier, but it also provides the ability to have different versions on a per-route basis. And, it also provides support for the *Accept-version* header to pick the right route.

Note   If the header is missing, and more than one version for the same route is available, then Restify will pick the first one defined in the code.

Listing 5-17 shows how to do it.

Listing 5-17. Route Versioning with Restify

```
function respV1(req, res, next) {
  res.send("This is version 1.0.2")
}
function respV2(req, res, next) {
  res.send("This is version 2.1.3")
}
let  myPath = "/my/route"
server.get({path: myPath, version: "1.0.2"},  respV1)
server.get({path: myPath, version: "2.1.3"},  respV2)
```

Now, when hitting the path with different values for Accept-version, the information in Table 5-6 is what you get.

Table 5-6. *Examples of Content Negotiation*

Version Used	Response	Description
	This is version 1.0.2	No version was used, so by default, the server is picking the first one defined.
~1	This is version 1.0.2	Version 1.x.x was selected, so that is what the server responds with.

~3	{
	"code": "InvalidVersion",
	"message": "GET /my/route
	supports versions: 1.0.2, 2.1.3"
	}
		An error message is returned when an unsupported version is requested.

Content Negotiation

Another interesting feature that Restify provides is support for content negotiation.

All you need to do to implement this feature is provide the right content formatters during initialization, like in Listing 5-18.

Listing 5-18. Content Negotiation Example

```
restify.createServer({
  formatters: {
    'application/foo; q=0.9': (req, res, body) => {
      if (body instanceof Error)
        return body.stack;

      if (Buffer.isBuffer(body))
        return body.toString('base64');

      return util.inspect(body);
    }
  }
})
```

Note   By default, Restify comes bundled with formatters for application/json, text/plain, and application/octet-stream.

There are other minor features provided by Restify that I'm not covering, so please refer to the official web site for information.

Vatican.js

Vatican.js is an attempt at creating an easy-to-use and boilerplate-based library, which can reduce the coding time while working on RESTful APIs. When you're starting to work on your API's code, there are a lot of repeated tasks that you need to perform over and over, until you have all your endpoints set up, and your models, and so on. This library attempts to remove all that work by generating most of it automatically. Table 5-7 shows more details about the framework.

Table 5-7.   *Vatican.js Module Information*

Category	Request/Response handler, Middleware, Routes handling
Current version	1.5.0
Description	Vatican.js is another attempt of a framework designed to create RESTful APIs. It doesn't follow the Express/Restify path. Its focus is more on the MVP stage of the API, but it provides an interesting alternative.
Home page URL	`https://github.com/deleteman/vatican`
Installation	`$ npm install -g vatican`

Code Examples

After installation, Vatican.js provides a command-line script to create the project and add resources and resource handlers to it. So to get the project started, you'll need to use the following command:

```
$ vatican new test_project
```

The preceding code generates the output shown in Figure 5-3.

```
New project started:
Creating /home/fernando/workspace/writing/node/test_project ...
Creating /home/fernando/workspace/writing/node/test_project/./handlers ...
Creating /home/fernando/workspace/writing/node/test_project/vatican-conf.json ...
Creating /home/fernando/workspace/writing/node/test_project/index.js ...
Creating /home/fernando/workspace/writing/node/test_project/package.json ...

 Project files created, now just follow these steps:
1- cd into your new project folder
2- npm install
3- node index.js
```

Figure 5-3. *Output of the Vatican.js generate action*

The main file (`index.js`) has the content in Listing 5-19.

Listing 5-19. Default index.js Generated by Vatican.js.

```
var Vatican = require("vatican")

//Use all default settings
var app = new Vatican()

app.dbStart(function() {
    console.log("Db connection stablished...")

    //Start the server
    app.start()
} )
```

Vatican comes with MongoDB integration, so the `dbStart` method is actually a reference to the connection to the NoSQL storage. By default, the server is assumed to be in *localhost* and the database name used is `vatican-project`.

The default port for Vatican is 8753, but just like all defaults in Vatican, it can be overwritten during the instantiation stage. These are the options that can be passed in to the constructor, as shown in Table 5-8.

Table 5-8. *List of Options for the Vatican.js Constructor*

Option	Description
port	Port of the HTTP server
handlers	Path to the folder where all handlers are stored. By default it's `./handlers`
db	Object with two attributes: host and dbname
cors	This is either a Boolean indicating whether CORS is supported by the API or an object indicating each of the supported headers.

Setting up a route in Vatican is also a bit different than the others; the command-line script provides the ability to autogenerate the code for the entity/model file and the controller/handler file, which also includes basic code for the CRUD operations.

To autogenerate the code, use the following command from within the project's folder:

```
$ vatican g Books -a title:string description:string copies:int -m
newBook:post listBooks:get removeBook:delete
```

This line outputs something like what's shown in Figure 5-4.

```
File written in: /home/fernando/workspace/writing/node/test_project/schemas/Books.js
File written in: ./handlers/Books.js
```

Figure 5-4. *Output of the resource generator command*

It basically means that Vatican created both the handler file and the entity (inside the schemas folder). If you check the handler's file, you'll notice how all the actions already have their code in there; that's because Vatican was able to guess the meaning of the actions provided in the command line by using their name.

- newBook: Using "new" assumes you're creating a new instance of the resource.

- listBooks: Using "list" assumes you want to generate a list of items.

- removeBook: Using "remove" assumes you're trying to remove a resource.

Variations of those words are also valid, and Vatican will use them to guess the code. You can now go ahead and start the server; the endpoints will work and save information to the database.

One final comment on resource generation is about routing; you haven't specified any routes yet, but Vatican has created them anyway. Inside the handler file, you'll notice annotations as shown in Listing 5-20.

Listing 5-20. Generated Code for New REST Methods with Endpoint Definition Included

```
module.exports = class BooksHdlr {

        constructor(model, dbModels) {
                this.model = model;
                this.dbModels = dbModels;
        }

        @endpoint (url: /books method: post)
        newBook(req, res, next) {
                var data = req.params.body
                //...maybe do validation here?
                this.model.create(data, function(err, obj) {
                        if(err) return next(err)
                        res.send(obj)
                })
        }

        @endpoint (url: /books method: get)
        listBooks(req, res, next) {
                var page = null,
                        size = null
                if(req.params.query.page || req.params.query.size) {
                        page = req.params.query.page || 0
                        size = req.params.query.size || 10
                }
```

```
        var query = {}

        var finder = this.model.find(query)

        if(page !== null && size !== null) {
                finder
                        .skip(page * size)
                        .limit(size)
        }

        finder.exec(function(err, list) {
                if(err) return next(err)
                res.send(list)
        })
    }

@endpoint (url: /books method: delete)
removeBook(req, res, next) {
        var id = req.params.query.id || req.params.url.id ||
        req.params.body.id

        this.model.remove({_id: id}, function(err) {
                if(err) return next(err)
                res.send({success: true})
        });
    }

}
```

The annotations in the preceding example on the method's definition are not standard JavaScript, but Vatican is able to parse them and turn them into data during boot up. That means that with Vatican there is no routes file; each route is defined above its associated method, and if you want to get a full list of routes for your system, you can use the following command line:

```
$ vatican list
```

And it'll produce the output shown in Figure 5-5, which lists for every handler all the routes with the method, the path, the file, and the associated method name.

```
2014-12-31T05:18:16.468Z - info: Openning file: ./handlers/Books.js
List of routes found:
[POST] /books -> ./handlers/Books.js::newBook
[GET] /books -> ./handlers/Books.js::listBooks
[DELETE] /books -> ./handlers/Books.js::removeBook
```

Figure 5-5. *Output from the list command*

Note   The annotations can be commented out with a single line comment (//) to avoid your editor/linter from complaining about the construct; even then, Vatican.js will be able to parse it.

Finally, Vatican also fits inside the middleware category, and that's because even though it's not based on Connect or Express, it does support Connect-based middleware. The only difference is the method name that uses it.

Listing 5-21. Middleware Usage Example

```
vatican.preprocess(middlewareFunction) //generic middleware for all routes
vatican.preprocess(middelwareFunction, ['login', 'authentication'])
//middleware for two routes: login and authentication.
```

To set the name of a route, you can add that parameter in the annotation, like in Listing 5-22.

Listing 5-22. Setting Up Named Routes Using Annotations

```
@endpoint(url: /path method: get name: login)
```

There are still some more features that Vatican.js provides. To read about them, please refer to the official web site.

swagger-node-express

This module bridges the gap between Swagger and Express, allowing you to auto-document your express APIs easily. Table 5-9 shows more details about it.

Table 5-9. *swagger-node-express Module Information*

Category	Up-to-date documentation
Current version	2.1.3
Description	This is a module for Express. It integrates into an Express app and provides the functionalities that Swagger[3] does for documenting APIs, which is a web interface with documentation of each method and the ability to try these methods.
Home page URL	`https://github.com/swagger-api/swagger-node`
Installation	`$ npm install swagger-node-express`

Code Examples

The first thing you need to do after you install the module is integrate Swagger into your Express app. Listing 5-23 provides the code to do that.

Listing 5-23. First Steps After Installing swagger-node-express

```
// Load module dependencies.
const express = require("express")
, app = express()
, bodyParser = require("body-parser")
, swagger = require("swagger-node-express").createNew(app);

// Create the application.
app.use(express.json());
app.use(bodyParser.urlencoded({extended: true}));
```

After integration is done, the next thing to do is add the models and the handlers. The models are in the form of JSON data (where this is defined is left to the preference of the developer). The handlers contain the actual code of the route handlers, along with other descriptive fields that act as documentation.

---

[3]See `http://swagger.io/`.

Listing 5-24 is an example of a model definition.

Listing 5-24. Model Definition Using Simple JSON Format

```
exports.models = {
        "Book": {
                "id": "Book",
                "required": ["title", "isbn"],
                "properties": {
                        "title": {
                                "type": "string",
                                "description": "The title of the book"
                        },
                        "isbn": {
                                "type": "string",
                                "description": "International Standard
                                Book Number"
                        },
                        "copies": {
                                "type": "integer",
                                "format": "int64",
                                "description": "Number of copies of the
                                book owned by the bookstore"
                        }
                }
        }
}
```

In Listing 5-24, the format used is JSON Schema[4] and it might be tedious to maintain, but it provides a standard way for Swagger to understand how our models are created.

---

[4]See http://json-schema.org/.

> **Tip** Manually maintaining a lot of model descriptions might be too much work, and it's prone to generate errors in the documentation, so it might be a good idea to either use the description to autogenerate the code of the model or autogenerate the description from the model's code.

Once the model description is done, you add it to Swagger, as deomstrated in Listing 5-25.

Listing 5-25. Letting Swagger Know About Your Models

```
// Load module dependencies.
const express = require("express")
, swagger = require("swagger-node-express")
, models = require('./models-definitions').models
//....
```

swagger.addModels(models)

Now you move on to the handler's description, which contains fields describing each method, and the actual code to execute.

Listing 5-26. Handler's Code and Documentation Definition and Setup

```
const swagger = require("swagger-node-express");
//Book handler's file
exports.listBooks = {
        "spec": {
                "description": "Returns the list of books",
                "path": "/books.{format}",
                "method": "GET",
                "type": "Book",
                "nickname": "listBooks",
                "produces": ["application/json"],
                "parameters": [swagger.paramTypes.query("sortBy",
                "Sort books by title or isbn", "string")]
```

```
    },
    "action": (req, res) => {
        //...
    }
}

//main file's code
var bookHandler = require("./bookHandler")
//...
swagger.addGet(bookHandler.listBooks) // adds the handler for the list
action and the actual action itself
```

This code shows how to describe a specific service (a list of books). Again, some of these parameters (inside the spec object) can be autogenerated; otherwise, manually maintaining a lot of specs can lead to outdated documentation.

Finally, set up the URLs for the Swagger UI (which will display the documentation and will also provide the UI to test the API) and the version, as shown in Listing 5-27.

Listing 5-27. Letting Swagger Know Its UI's URL

```
swagger.configure("http://myserver.com", "0.1")
```

Let's now look at Listing 5-28, a complete example of a main file, showing the setup and configuration of Swagger and the Swagger UI.[5]

Listing 5-28. Full Example of Swagger-Express Integration

```
// Load module dependencies.
const express = require("express")
, models = require("./models-definitions").models
, app = express()
, bodyParser = require("body-parser")
, booksHandler = require("./booksHandler") //load the handler's definition
, swagger = require("swagger-node-express").createNew(app) //bundle the app
to swagger
```

---

[5]See https://github.com/swagger-api/swagger-ui.

```
// Create the application.
app.use(express.json());
app.use(bodyParser.urlencoded({extended: true}));

var static_url = express.static(__dirname + '/swagger-ui') //the swagger-ui
is inside the "swagger-ui" folder

swagger.configureSwaggerPaths("", "api-docs", "") //you remove the {format}
part of the paths, to simplify things
app.get(/^\/docs(\/.*)?$/ ,  (req, res, next) => {
    if(req.url === '/docs') {
        res.writeHead(302, {location: req.url + "/"})
        res.end()
        return
    }

    req.url = req.url.substr('/docs'.length)
    return static_url(req, res, next)
})

//add the models and the handler
swagger
    .addModels(models)
    .addGet(booksHandler.listBooks)

swagger.configure("http://localhost:3000", "1.0.0")
app.listen("3000")
```

Note   Before trying out this code, you'll have to copy the folder called "swagger-ui" inside the module's folder, into your project's root folder (or whatever you set the *static_url* variable to).

Figure 5-6 is a screenshot of the resulting UI that you get by visiting
`http://localhost:3000/docs`.

[BASE URL: http://localhost:3000/api-docs , API VERSION: 1.0.0]

Figure 5-6. *The generated UI*

I/ODocs

Another option when it comes to self-documenting APIs is I/O Docs, which, although in the end provides similar results to Swagger, also offers quite a different approach getting there.

Table 5-10 shows the details on this particular project, as well as the steps required to install it.

Table 5-10. *I/O Docs Module Information*

Category	Up-to-date documentation
Current Version	N/A
Description	I/O Docs is a live documentation system designed for RESTful APIs. By defining the API using the JSON Schema, I/O Docs generates a web interface to try out the API.
Home page URL	`https://github.com/mashery/iodocs`

Installation	$ git clone http://github.com/mashery/iodocs.git
	$ cd iodocs
	$ npm install

Code Examples

After installation is done, the only thing left to do to test the application is create a configuration file; there is a `config.json.sample` file you can use as a starting point.

Tip   You can copy the config.json.sample file using the cp command like so: cp
config.json.sample config.json . By doing that, you immediately have a
valid config file to start using.

To start up the documentation server, you'll first need to start your redis server and then use one of the following commands:

```
$ redis-server #preferabliy you'll do this in another console, since this
is a blocking operation
$ npm start        #for *nix and OSX systems
C:\your-project-folder> npm startwin        #for Windows systems
```

After that, use your browser to go to `http://localhost:3000` to start testing the documentation system.

> **Tip**   If you get a login modal the first time you visit that URL, just hit ENTER (with empty credentials) and you'll be logged in.

Figure 5-7 is a screenshot of one of the sample APIs already configured.

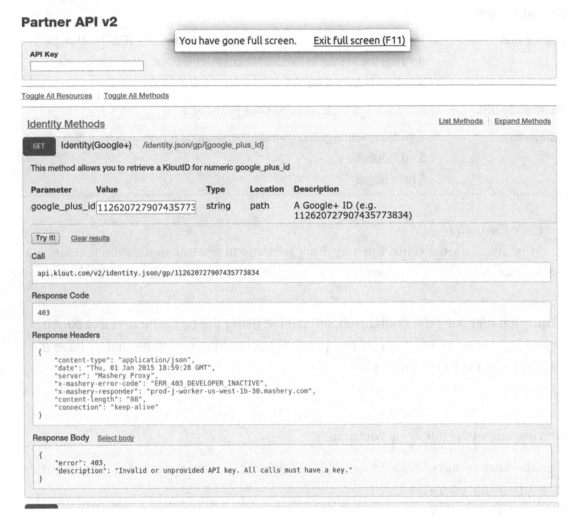

Figure 5-7. *The default UI when trying out methods*

As you can see in Figure 5-7, when the methods are tested, a response is shown underneath. If you want to set up your own API, there are a few things to do:

1. Add your API to the list of documented APIs inside `public/data/` `apiconfig.json` like in Listing 5-29.

Listing 5-29. Adding Your API's Entry to the List of Docummented APIs

```
{
    "klout": {
        "name": "Klout v2 API"
    },
    "egnyte": {
        "name": "Egnyte API"
    },
    "usatoday": {
        "name": "USA TODAY Census API"
    },
    "foursquare": {
        "name": "Foursquare (OAuth 2.0 Auth Code)"
    },
    "rdio": {
        "name": "Rdio Beta (OAuth 2.0 Client Credentials)"
    },
    "rdio2": {
        "name": "Rdio Beta (OAuth 2.0 Implicit Grant)"
    },
    "requestbin": {
        "name": "Requestb.in"
    },
    "bookstore": {
        "name": "Dummy Bookstore API"
    }
}
```

2. Create a new file called bookstore.json and store it inside the
    public/data folder. This new JSON file will contain the description
    of your API and the methods in it; something like shown in
    Listing 5-30.

Listing 5-30. The Full JSON Definition of Your API's Endpoints

```
{
    "name": "Dummy Bookstore API",
    "description": "Simple bookstore API",
    "protocol": "rest",
    "basePath": "http://api.mybookstore.com",
    "publicPath": "/v1",
    "auth": {
        "key": {
            "param": "key"
        }
    },
    "headers": {
        "Accept": "application/json",
        "Foo": "bar"
    },
    "resources": {
        "Books": {
            "methods": {
                "listBooks": {
                    "name": "List of books",
                    "path": "/books",
                    "httpMethod": "GET",
                    "description": "Returns the list of books in stock",
                    "parameters": {
                        "sortBy": {
                            "type": "string",
                            "required": false,
                            "default": "title",
                            "description": "Sort the results by title
                            or ISBN code"
                        }
                    }
                },
```

```
"showBook": {
    "name": "Show book",
    "path": "/books/{bookId}",
    "httpMethod": "GET",
    "description": "Returns the data of one specific book",
    "parameters": {
        "bookId": {
                "type": "string",
                "required": true,
                "default": "",
                "description": "The ID of the specific
                book"
            }
        }
    }
}
}
}
```

3. Start up the documentation server and point your web browser to it.
    You'll see a screen that looks similar to Figure 5-8.

Dummy Bookstore API

API Key

Toggle All Resources | Toggle All Methods

Books   List Methods | Expand Methods

GET   List of books   /books

Returns the list of books in stock

Parameter	Value	Type	Location	Description
sortBy	title	string	query	Sort the results by title or ISBN code

Try it!

GET   Show book   /books/{bookId}

Returns the data of one specific book

Parameter	Value	Type	Location	Description
bookId	required	string	query	The ID of the specific book

Try it!

©Mashery, Inc.   Powered by I/O Docs Community Edition

Figure 5-8. *Your custom documentation translated into a web UI*

Unlike with Swagger, this documentation system is not meant to be integrated into your project, so autogenerating the JSON code might be a bit more difficult. The server does, however, auto-adapt to updates on the JSON file, so you don't have to restart it everytime to change something, but you would still have to find a way to easily generate that JSON definition and copy it into the right folder.

Halson

Halson attempts to simplify the task of adding hypermedia into your response by providing an object-oriented interface. Table 5-11 shows the basic information about this module, including the steps to install it.

Table 5-11. *Halson Module Information*

Category	Hypermedia on the response
Current version	3.0.0
Description	Halson is a module that helps create HAL-compliant JSON objects, which you'll then be able to use as part of the response in your API.
Home page URL	`http://github.com/seznam/halson`
Installation	`$ npm install halson`

Code Examples

The API provided by this module is quite straightforward, and if you've read about the standard,[6] you should have no problem figuring out how to use it.

Listing 5-31 is the example from the readme.

Listing 5-31. Simple Halson Example

```
const halson = require('halson');

let embed = halson({
      title: "joyent / node",
      description: "evented I/O for v8 javascript"
   })
   .addLink('self', '/joyent/node')
   .addLink('author', {
      href: '/joyent',
      title: 'Joyent'
   });

let resource = halson({
      title: "Juraj Hájovský",
      username: "hajovsky",
```

---

[6]See `http://stateless.co/hal_specification.html`.

```
        emails: [
            "juraj.hajovsky@example.com",
            "hajovsky@example.com"
        ]
    })
    .addLink('self', '/hajovsky')
    .addEmbed('starred', embed);
console.log(JSON.stringify(resource));
```

The preceding code will output the following:

Listing 5-32. JSON Output Generated by HALSON

```json
{
  "title": "Juraj Hájovský",
  "username": "hajovsky",
  "emails": [
    "juraj.hajovsky@example.com",
    "hajovsky@example.com"
  ],
  "_links": {
    "self": {
      "href": "/hajovsky"
    }
  },
  "_embedded": {
    "starred": {
      "title": "joyent / node",
      "description": "evented I/O for v8 javascript",
      "_links": {
        "self": {
          "href": "/joyent/node"
        },
```

```
    "author": {
      "href": "/joyent",
      "title": "Joyent"
    }
  }
 }
}
```

As you can see, the module successfully abstracted the details about the HAL standard; all you need to know is how to add links and what an embedded object is.

HAL

Just like HALSON, this module creates the representation of Hypermedia linking your resources, which can then be added to your own API's response.

You can read the basic information about the module in Table 5-12.

Table 5-12. *HAL Module Information*

Category	Hypermedia on the response
Current version	1.2.0
Description	HAL is an alternative to HALSON. It provides a simpler interface but the same underlying functionality: abstracting the HAL+JSON format and giving the developer an easy way to use it.
Home page URL	https://www.npmjs.com/package/hal
Installation	$ npm install hal

Code Examples

The API of this module is simpler than the one provided by HALSON and it also provides XML encoding (remember that even though you're not focusing on XML, it can be a possible second representation for your resources).

Listing 5-33 provides a simple example following our bookstore theme.

Listing 5-33. Simple Example of Adding a List of Objects Embedded into a Parent

```
const hal = require('hal');

let books = new hal.Resource({name: "Books list"}, "/books")

let listOfBooks = [
  new hal.Resource({id: 1, title: "Harry Potter and the Philosopher's
  stone", copies: 3}, "/books/1"),
  new hal.Resource({id: 2, title: "Harry Potter and the Chamber of
  Secrets", copies: 5}, "/books/2"),
  new hal.Resource({id: 3, title: "Harry Potter and the Prisoner of
  Azkaban", copies: 6}, "/books/3"),
  new hal.Resource({id: 4, title: "Harry Potter and the Goblet of Fire",
  copies: 1}, "/books/4"),
  new hal.Resource({id: 5, title: "Harry Potter and the Order of the
  Phoenix", copies: 8}, "/books/5"),
  new hal.Resource({id: 6, title: "Harry Potter and the Half-blood Prince",
  copies: 2}, "/books/6"),
  new hal.Resource({id: 7, title: "Harry Potter and the Deathly Hollows",
  copies: 7},"/books/7")
]
books.embed('books', listOfBooks)
console.log(JSON.stringify(books.toJSON()))
```

This code will output the JSON code in Listing 5-34.

Listing 5-34. The JSON Representation of the Relationships Defined in the Previous Listing

```
{
  "_links": {
    "self": {
      "href": "/books"
    }
  },
```

```
"_embedded": {
  "books": [
    {
      "_links": {
        "self": {
          "href": "/books/1"
        }
      },
      "id": 1,
      "title": "Harry Potter and the Philosopher's stone",
      "copies": 3
    },
    {
      "_links": {
        "self": {
          "href": "/books/2"
        }
      },
      "id": 2,
      "title": "Harry Potter and the Chamber of Secrets",
      "copies": 5
    },
    {
      "_links": {
        "self": {
          "href": "/books/3"
        }
      },
      "id": 3,
      "title": "Harry Potter and the Prisoner of Azkaban",
      "copies": 6
    },
```

```json
  {
    "_links": {
      "self": {
        "href": "/books/4"
      }
    },
    "id": 4,
    "title": "Harry Potter and the Goblet of Fire",
    "copies": 1
  },
  {
    "_links": {
      "self": {
        "href": "/books/5"
      }
    },
    "id": 5,
    "title": "Harry Potter and the Order of the Phoenix",
    "copies": 8
  },
  {
    "_links": {
      "self": {
        "href": "/books/6"
      }
    },
    "id": 6,
    "title": "Harry Potter and the Half-blood Prince",
    "copies": 2
  },
  {
    "_links": {
      "self": {
        "href": "/books/7"
      }
    },
```

```
        "id": 7,
        "title": "Harry Potter and the Deathly Hollows",
        "copies": 7
      }
    ]
  },
  "name": "Books list"
}
```

JSON-Gate

JSON validation is useful to ensure that both the requests your API gets and the responses it provides are always in check against a publicly defined standard. This is where you can turn to JSON-Gate for help (please see Table 5-13 for basic information about the module).

Table 5-13. *JSON-Gate Module Information*

Category	Request/Response validation
Current version	0.8.23
Description	This module validates the structure and content of a JSON object against a predefined schema that follows the JSON Schema format.
Home page URL	https://www.npmjs.com/package/json-gate
Installation	$ npm install json-gate

Code Examples

The usage of this module is quite simple. First, you need to define the schema against which your objects will be validated. This can be done directly with the createSchema method or (recommended) in a separate file, and then passed to the validator. After the schema has been added, you can proceed to validate as many objects as you need.

Listing 5-35 provides a simple example.

Listing 5-35. Simple Example Showing how to Define a Schema and Validate Your Input Against It

```
const createSchema = require('json-gate').createSchema;

let schema = createSchema({
    type: 'object',
    properties: {
        title: {
            type: 'string',
            minLength: 1,
            maxLength: 64,
            required: true
        },
        copies: {
            type: 'integer',
            maximum: 20,
            default: 1
        },
        isbn: {
            type: 'integer',
            required: true
        }
    },
    additionalProperties: false
});

let invalidInput = {
    title: "This is a valid long title for a book, it might not be the best
    choice!",
    copies: "3"
}
```

```
try {
    schema.validate(invalidInput);
} catch(err) {
    return console.log(err)
}
```

The code from Listing 5-33 will output the following error:

```
[Error: JSON object property 'title': length is 71 when it should be at
most 64]
```

There are two things to note here:

- On one hand, the error message is very "human-friendly." All the error messages reported by JSON-Gate are like this, so it's easy to understand what you did wrong.

- On the other hand, as you probably noticed, the invalidInput object has three errors in its format (exceeding length of the title parameter, invalid type for the copies parameter, and finally, a missing isbn parameter); the validation stops at the first error, so correcting multiple problems might be slow because you'll have to correct them one at a time.

If you're not into catching exceptions (and why should you in Node.js?), there is an alternative to the validate method, which is passing in a second argument—a callback function with two arguments: the error object and the original input object.

TV4

Just like with the previous module, this one empowers you with the ability to validate your input and output messages easily. Table 5-14 has all the infomation you need to get you started using TV4.

Table 5-14. *TV4 Module Information*

Category	Request/Response validation
Current version	1.3.0
Description	This module provides validation against version 4 of the JSON Schema.[7]
Home page url	`https://www.npmjs.com/package/tv4`
Installation	`$ npm install tv4`

Code Examples

The main difference between this validator and JSON-Gate is that this one is specific for version 4 of the JSON Schema draft. It also allows you to collect multiple errors during validation and to reference other schemas, so you can reuse parts of the schema in different sections.

Let's look at some examples:

Listing 5-36. Simple Example of Input Validation Using TV4

```
var  validator = require("tv4")

var schema ={
    "title": "Example Schema",
    "type": "object",
    "properties": {
        "firstName": {
            "type": "string"
        },
        "lastName": {
            "type": "string"
        },
        "age": {
            "description": "Age in years",
            "type": "integer",
```

---

[7]See `http://json-schema.org/latest/json-schema-core.html`.

```
            "minimum": 0
        }
    },
    "required": ["firstName", "lastName"]
}

var invalidInput = {
    firstName: 42,
    age: "100"
}

var results = validator.validateMultiple(invalidInput, schema)
console.log(results)
```

The preceding example will output the following error object:

Listing 5-37. Multiple Error Messages Returned by the Code from Listing 5-34

```
{ errors:
  [ { message: 'Missing required property: lastName',
      params: [Object],
      code: 302,
      dataPath: '',
      schemaPath: '/required/1',
      subErrors: null,
      stack: '......'},
    { message: 'Invalid type: number (expected string)',
      params: [Object],
      code: 0,
      dataPath: '/firstName',
      schemaPath: '/properties/firstName/type',
      subErrors: null,
      stack: '......'},
    { message: 'Invalid type: string (expected integer)',
      params: [Object],
      code: 0,
      dataPath: '/age',
```

```
      schemaPath: '/properties/age/type',
      subErrors: null,
      stack: '......'}]
  missing: [],
  valid: false }
```

The output is much bigger than the one from JSON-Gate and it needs a bit of parsing before being able to use it, but it also provides quite a lot of information aside from the simple error message.

For a full reference on the API provided by this validator, please visit its home page. To understand all the possible validations that can be done using JSON Schema, please visit the online draft.[8]

Summary

This chapter covered a lot of modules that will help you create the perfect API architecture. You saw at least two modules for every category on options for picking the tools for the job.

In the next chapter, you'll define the API that you'll be developing in the following chapters, and with that definition, you'll also pick the set of modules (from the ones we covered in this chapter) that you'll use to develop it.

---

[8]See http://json-schema.org/specification.html.

CHAPTER 6

Planning Your REST API

You're almost ready to get your hands dirty and start developing the actual API; but before you start, let's apply everything I've talked about until this point:

- REST

- Defining what an ideal RESTful architecture should look like

- Good practices when developing an API

- Modules that would help achieve that ideal goal

In this chapter, I'll set up the ground work for the final development this book will take you through:

- I'll define a specific problem to solve.

- You'll create a written specification for it, writing down the list of resources and endpoints.

- To help understand how all those resources relate to each other, you'll create a UML diagram of our system.

- I'll go over some options for a database engine, choosing the best one for our problem.

The final result of this chapter will be all the information you need to start the development process (covered in the next chapter).

The Problem

In case you haven't noticed yet, throughout this book, every major (and probably minor, too) code sample and fake scenario has been done using a bookstore as the root of that example. This chapter keeps up that trend, so instead of switching into another area, you'll dig deeper and flesh-out our fake bookstore.

173

© Fernando Doglio 2018
F. Doglio, *REST API Development with Node.js*, https://doi.org/10.1007/978-1-4842-3715-1_6

Let's call our fake bookstore Come&Read and assume that we've been asked to create a distributed API that will bring the bookstore into the twenty-first century.

Right now, it's a pretty decent business. The bookstore currently has 10 different points of sale located across the United States—not a lot, but the company leadership is considering expanding into even more states. The current main problem, though, is that all of those stores have barely entered the digital era. The way of working and recordkeeping is very manual and heterogeneous; for instance:

- Some of the smaller stores keep records on paper and send a manually typed weekly report to the head store.

- While the bigger locations tend to use some sort of CRM software, there is no standard as long as numbers are exported into a common format and sent in a weekly report.

- Based on the weekly reports, the head store handles inventory of the chain-wide matters (store-specific stock, global stock, sales both per-store and global, employee records, etc.).

- Overall, the bookstore lacks web interaction with its customers, which a twenty-first century business must have. Its web site only lists addresses and phone numbers, and nothing more.

Figure 6-1 shows an image mapping the current situation of this bookstore chain.

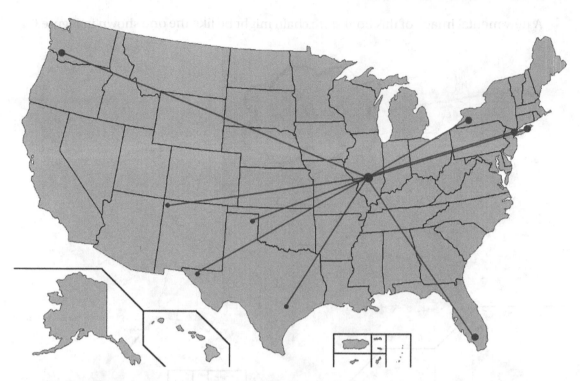

Figure 6-1. *How every store connects to the main store*

As you can see in Figure 6-1, all of the secondary stores are connected by a very thin line to the main store, which is located in Springfield, IL.

The goal is to grow as a business not only by opening new stores across the country but by also strengthening the bond between all the stores. And to achieve this, the backbone of everything will be our API. Our system will have to be a decentralized one, meaning that you'll treat the main store just like any other store and provide a common set of tools and data sources for every client application that might come in the future, instantly allowing for such things as the following:

- Cross-store searches

- Automatic control of global stock

- Automatic control over sales on a global level

- Dynamic data sources for things like web sites and mobile apps

A new mental image of this bookstore chain might be like the one shown in Figure 6-2.

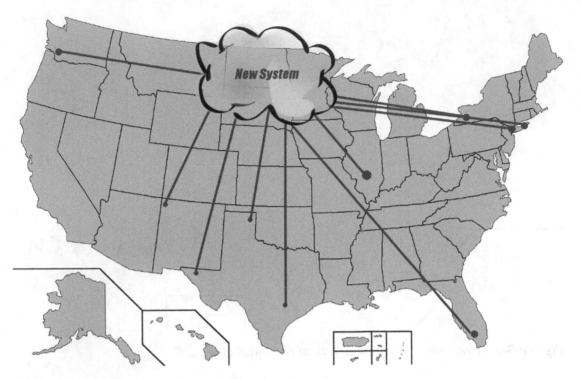

Figure 6-2. *The new status of the bookstore chain*

Figure 6-2 shows the new system living in the cloud, with all stores connected directly to it. The bond is stronger now, since everything is done automatically and every piece of information is available to all stores. Also, this new API-based system allows for the easy development of new ways to interact with potential customers, including mobile apps and dynamic web sites.

The Specifications

Now that we know the current situation of the chain and the goal of our system, we need to start writing some hard specs. These will determine the way the system evolves and help with planning the development by giving us a better idea of the size of the project. Specifications also help us spot any design errors before we start with the implementation.

Note   We will not spend much time on the process of writing the system's specs, since that subject is beyond the scope of this book. We'll just lay down the specs and note anything that might be extremely relevant; the rest will be left to your understanding of this process.

To provide everything mentioned, the system needs to have the following features:

- *Cross-store book search/listing capabilities.*

- *Storage*: This code is in charge of providing the information to all other entities, as well as talking directly to the data storage system that you choose.

- *Sales*: This feature is dedicated to allow for both in-store and online sales.

- *User reviews of books*: This will provide a much-needed layer of interaction between the stores and the potential clients.

- *Authentication*: This will let employees and customers login into the system.

Table 6-1 describes the resources that we'll be dealing with in this implementation.

Table 6-1. *Resources, Properties, and Basic Descriptions*

Resource	Properties	Description
Books	• Title • Authors • ISBN Code • Stores • Genre • Description • Reviews • Price	This is the main entity; it has all the properties required to identify a book and to locate it in a specific store.
Authors	• Name • Description • Books • Website • Image/Avatar	This resource is highly related to a book's resource because it lists the author of every book in a store.
Stores	• Name • Address • State • Phone numbers • Employees	Basic information about each store, including the address, employees, and so forth.
Employees	• First name • Last name • Birthdate • Address • Phone numbers • Email • HireDate • EmployeeNumber • Store	Employee information, contact data, and other internal properties that may come in handy for an admin type of user.

(continued)

Table 6-1. (*continued*)

Resource	Properties	Description
Clients	• Name • Address • Phone number • Email	Basic contact information about a client.
BookSales	• Date • Books • Store • Employee • Client • TotalAmount	The record of a book sale. It can be related to a store sale or an online sale.
ClientReviews	• Client • Book • ReviewText • Stars	The resource in which client reviews about a book are saved. The client can enter a short free-text review and a number between 0 and 5 to represent stars.

Note   Even though it's not listed in Table 6-1, all resources will have some database-related attributes, such as id, created_at, and updated_at, which you'll use throughout the code.

Based on the resources in Table 6-1, let's create a new table that lists the endpoints needed for each resource. Table 6-2 helps define the functionalities that each resource will have associated to it.

Table 6-2. *List of Endpoints, Associated Parameters, and HTTP Methods*

Endpoint	Attributes	Method	Description
/books	q: Optional search term. genre: Optional filtering by book genre. Defaults to "all."	GET	Lists and searches all books. If the q parameter is present, it's used as a free-text search; otherwise, the endpoint can be used to return lists of books by genre.
/books		POST	Creates a new book and saves it in the database
/books/:id		GET	Returns information about a specific book
/books/:id		PUT	Updates the information on a book
/books/:id/ authors		GET	Returns the author(s) of a specific book
/books/:id/ reviews		GET	Returns user reviews for a specific book
/authors	genre: Optional; defaults to "all." q: Optional search term	GET	Returns a list of authors. If genre is present, it's used to filter by the type of book published. If q is present, it's used to do a free- text search on the author's information.
/authors		POST	Adds a new author
/authors/:id		PUT	Updates the data on a specific author
/authors/:id		GET	Returns the data on a specific author
/authors/:id/ books		GET	Returns a list of books written by a specific author
/stores	state: Optional; filters the list of stores by state name.	GET	Returns the list of stores
/stores		POST	Adds a new store to the system
/stores/:id		GET	Returns the data on a specific store

(continued)

Table 6-2. (*continued*)

Endpoint	Attributes	Method	Description
/stores/:id/ books	q: Optional; does a full-text search of books within a specific store. genre: Optional; filters the results by genre.	GET	Returns a list of books that are in stock at a specific store. If the attribute q is used, it performs a full-text search on those books
/stores/:id/ employees		GET	Returns a list of the employees working at a specific store
/stores/:id/ booksales		GET	Returns a list of the sales at a specific store
/stores/:id		PUT	Updates the information about a specific store
/employees		GET	Returns a full list of the employees working across all stores
/employees		POST	Adds a new employee to the system
/ employees/:id		GET	Returns the data on a specific employee
/ employees/:id		PUT	Updates the data on a specific employee
/clients		GET	Lists clients ordered alphabetically by name
/clients		POST	Adds a new client to the system
/clients/:id		GET	Returns the data on a specific client
/clients/:id		PUT	Updates the data on a specific client

(*continued*)

Table 6-2. (*continued*)

Endpoint	Attributes	Method	Description
/booksales	start_date: Filters records that were created after this date. end_date: Optional; filters records that were created before this date. store_id: Optional; filters records by store.	GET	Returns a list of sales. The results can be filtered by time range or by store.
/booksales		POST	Records a new book sale
/clientreviews		POST	Saves a new client review of a book

Tip   Even though they're not specified, all endpoints that deal with listing resources will accept the following attributes: page (starting at 0, the page number to return); perpage (the number of items per page to return); and a special attribute called sort, which contains the field name by which to sort the results and the order in the following format: [FIELD_NAME]_[ASC|DESC] (e.g., title_asc).

Table 6-2 gives us a pretty good idea of the size of the project; with it we're able to estimate the amount of work that we have ahead of us.

There is one more aspect to discuss because it isn't covered in the resources in Table 6-1 or with the endpoints/authentication in Table 6-2.

The authentication scheme will be simple. As discussed in Chapter 2, we'll use the *stateless* alternative by signing every request with a MAC (message authentication code). The server will re-create that code to verify that the request is actually valid. This means there will not be a signing process embedded into our system; that can be done by the client. No need to worry about that for now.

Note   Since it's not part of the scope of this book, the API will not handle charging for the book sales. This means that we'll assume that the book sale was done outside of our system, and that another system will post the results into our API to keep a record of it. In a production system, this is a good way to handle this functionality inside the API itself, thus providing a complete solution.

Keeping Track of Stock per Store

Table 6-1 shows that every book tracks the stores at which it is being sold. It is not completely clear, however, what happens if there is more than one copy of the same book per store.

To keep track of this number, let's enhance the relation between the books and the stores models by assigning another element: the number of copies. You'll see this in a bit in the UML diagram, but this is how the system will keep global stock of every book.

UML Diagram

With the level of specification we have so far, we could very well skip this step and jump right into the next one; but for the sake of completeness and getting a clear idea across, let's create a basic UML diagram to provide another way to show how all of the resources of the API will relate to each other.

As you can see in Figure 6-3, most of the diagram consists of groups of aggregations between different resources. The store has a group for employees, a group for books, a group for the books' authors (usually it's one author per book, but there are books that are co-authored by two or more authors), and a group for client reviews.

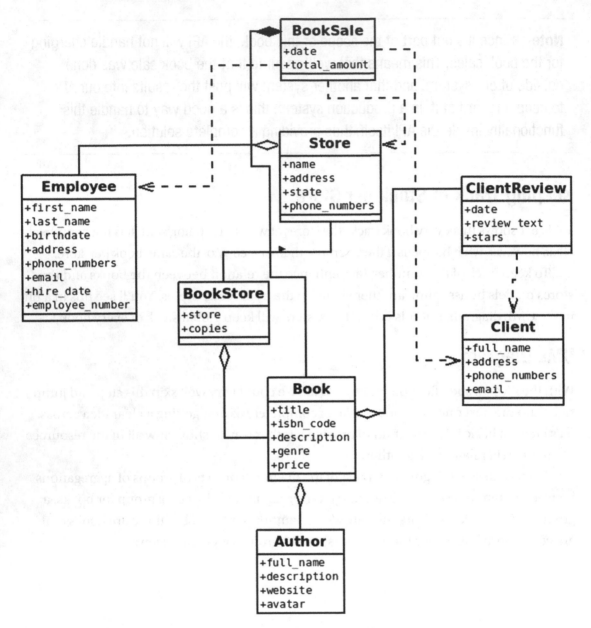

Figure 6-3. UML diagram showing the relations between all resources

Choosing a Database Storage System

It's time to stop writing lists of endpoints and creating diagrams; you need to start picking technologies. In this case, I'll go over some of the most common choices for a database storage system. I'll talk a bit about each one and we'll decide on one of them.

The bottom line is that all the solutions are valid—you could very well go with any of them, but we'll need to choose one in the end, so let's define what it is needed in the database system:

- *Speed of development*: Because you want the process to go quickly and not have interaction with the database be a bottleneck, you need something that integrates easily.

- *Easy-to-change schema*: With everything predefined, you have a pretty solid idea of what the schema is going to look like, but you might want to adjust things during development. It's always better if the storage you're using allows for this without a lot of hustle.

- *Ability to handle entity relations*: This means that key/value stores are out of the question.

- *Seamless integration between the entities' code and the database representation of the data.*

That's pretty much about it. In this case, we want something that can be integrated fast, changed easily, and is not key/value.

Therefore, the options are as follows:

- MySQL[1]: A classic choice when it comes to relational databases.

- PostgreSQL[2]: Another great choice when it comes to relational database engines.

- MongoDB[3]: A document-based NoSQL database engine.

So, now that you have our list of options, let's analyze how well each one of them complies with our requirements.

---

[1]See http://mysql.com/.

[2]See http://www.postgresql.org/.

[3]See http://www.mongodb.org/.

Fast Integration

Integration with the system means how easily the modules interact with the specific database engine. With MySQL and PostgreSQL, there is Sequelize,[4] which provides very complete and powerful object-relational mapping (ORM). It lets you focus more on the data model than on the actual engine particularities. Besides, if you use it right, you can potentially switch between both engines with minimum impact on the code.

On the other hand, with MongoDB you have Mongoose.js,[5] which allows you to abstract your code from the engine, simplifying your task when it comes to defining the schemas, validations, and so forth.

Easy-to-Change Schemas

This time around, the fixed structure provided by both MySQL and PostgreSQL makes it harder to maintain dynamic schemas, so every time you make a change, you'll need to update the schema by running migrations.

The lack of structure provided by the NoSQL engines makes MongoDB the perfect choice for our project, because making a change on the schema is as simple as making the changes on the definition code—no migration or anything else required.

Ability to Handle Entity Relations

Since we're leaving out key/value stores like Redis,[6] all of our three options are able to handle entity relations. Both MySQL and PostgreSQL are especially good at this, since they're both *relational* database engines. But let's not rule out MongoDB; it is *document-*based NoSQL storage, which in turn allows you to have documents (that translate directly into a MySQL record) and subdocuments, which are a special kind of relation that we don't have with our relational options.

Subdocument relations help to simplify both schemas and queries when working with the data. You saw in Figure 6-3 that most of our relations are based on aggregation, so this might be a good way to solve that.

---

[4]See `http://sequelizejs.com/`.

[5]See `http://mongoosejs.com/`.

[6]See `http://redis.io`.

Seamless Integration Between Our Models and the Database Entities

This is more of a comparison between Sequelize and Mongoose. Since they both abstract the storage layer, you need compare how that abstraction affects this point.

Ideally, we want our entities (our resources' representations in the code) to be passed to our storage layer or to interact with the storage layer. We don't want to require an extra type of object, usually called a DTO (data transfer object), to transfer the state of our entities between layers.

Luckily, the entities provided by Sequelize and by Mongoose fall into this category, so we might as well call it a draw.

And the Winner Is...

We need to pick one, so let's summarize:

- *Fast integration*: Let's give this one to Sequelize, since it comes with the added bonus of being able to switch engines with minimum impact.

- *Easy-to-change schemas*: MongoDB wins this one, hands down.

- *Handling of entity relations*: I'd like to give this one to MongoDB as well, mainly due to the subdocuments feature.

- *Seamless integration with our data models*: This one is a draw, so we're not counting it.

The final result seems to point toward MongoDB, but it's a pretty close win, so in the end, personal experience needs to be taken into account as well. Personally, I find MongoDB to be a very interesting alternative when prototyping and creating something new, something that might change during the development process many times, but this is why we'll go with it for our development. This way there is the extra insurance that if we need to change something, like adapting our data model to a new structure, we can do so easily and with minor impact.

The obvious module choice here is Mongoose, which provides a layer of abstraction over the MongoDB driver.

Choosing the Right Modules for the Job

This is the last step of our preparation process. Now that you know the problem to solve and you have a pretty well-defined specification of how to handle the development, the only thing left to do, aside from actually coding, is to pick the right modules.

In Chapter 5, I went over a list of modules that would help us achieve a pretty complete RESTful system; so let's quickly pick some of them for this development:

- Restify will be the basis of everything we do. It'll provide the structure needed to handle and process the requests and to provide a response to them.

- Swagger will be used to create the documentation. In Chapter 5, I talked about swagger-node-express, but just like that, there is one that works with Restify called (unsurprisingly enough) swagger-node-restify.[7] This module was chosen because it integrates into our project, allowing us to autogenerate our documentation based on our original code, instead of having to maintain two different repositories.

- Halson will be our module of choice for adding hypermedia to our responses. Mainly chosen because it appears to be more mature than HAL (the other modules examined for this task).

- Finally, the validation of our JSONs will be done using TV4, mainly because it allows us to gather all validation errors at once.

Note   These are not the only modules that we'll use; there are other minor auxiliary modules that will help us in different situations, but the ones listed are the ones that will help us achieve a RESTful API.

---

[7]See https://www.npmjs.com/package/swagger-node-restify.

Summary

We now have all we need to start coding. We know the extent of the API for the bookstore chain that we'll develop. We have planned the internal architecture of the system and have chosen the main modules that we'll use.

In the next chapter, we'll start coding our API. By the end of the chapter, we should have a full-fledged working bookstore API.

CHAPTER 7

Developing Your REST API

Now that we have finally defined the tools that we'll use and the project that we'll develop with them, we're ready to actually start coding. This chapter will cover that part—from the organization of the files (the directory structure), through the small design decisions made during development, and finally the code itself.

This chapter will display the entire source code for the project, but we'll only go over the relevant parts. Sadly, some bits and pieces are just plain boring (like the JSON Schema definitions and the simpler models), so I'll skip it. These things should be pretty self-explanatory to developers anyway, no matter the level of expertise.

I'll cover the development stage as follows:

- Minor simplifications/design decisions made during development

- Folder structure, because it's always important to understand where everything is and why

- The code itself, file by file, including explanation when needed

---

Note   The code in this chapter is but one of the infinitely potential ways of solving the problem presented in Chapter 6. It attempts to show the concepts and modules mentioned throughout this book. It's also meant to show you only one potential development process, which tries to be agile and dynamic at the same time. Of course, there are different ways to go about the process, which may be better or worse for every reader.

191

© Fernando Doglio 2018
F. Doglio, *REST API Development with Node.js*, https://doi.org/10.1007/978-1-4842-3715-1_7

Minor Changes to the Plan

We spent two whole chapters going over different modules and planning the entire process to develop the API. We made some diagrams, and we even listed every resource and endpoint that we would need.

And yet, during development, the plan changes—not by a lot, but we still need to fine-tune some aspects of the design.

This isn't necessarily a bad thing, though. If the original plan changes significantly, then yes, that would mean we definitely did something wrong in the planning; but there is no escape from minor changes at this stage, unless you spend a lot more time in your design phase. I'm talking about going the whole nine yards here: writing detailed use cases with their corresponding edge conditions, flow charts—the works. That process, when done right and when followed by the team implementing the solution, most likely results in no changes during development. But for that to happen, we need a lot more time, and let's face it, aside from being the boring part of development (disclaimer: if you actually like that part better than developing, there's nothing wrong with you; I just haven't ever met anyone like you), it's not this book's focus either.

So we can play with the design, use the partial analysis and planning that we did in the previous chapter, and live with the consequences, which are very little, as you'll see.

Simplification of the Store–Employee Relationship

When I listed every resource, I said that the store would keep a list of employees and that each employee would keep a direct reference to the store. To maintain those relationships in MongoDB, however, means extra work. And since we don't really need this, we'll just keep the employees' records unaware of their assigned store and make sure that each store keeps up with the employees working in it.

Adding Swagger UI

I talked about Swagger back in Chapter 5, and I briefly mentioned Swagger UI, but I never really explained a lot. The Swagger UI project is the UI we'll use to test our API. The swagger-node-express and swagger-node-restify modules provide the back-end infrastructure that the UI needs; but without the Swagger UI project, we have nothing.

So, just download version 2.1.5 of this project from `https://github.com/swagger-api/swagger-ui/tree/v2.1.5` and add its dist folder into your project's root. I'll go over how to configure it in a bit.

Simplified Security

To simplify the security, we'll work under the premise that we're not really making a public API but rather an API for clients that are directly under our control.

That means that we will not require every client to request an access token with a limited life span. Instead, we'll work under the assumption that when we set up a new client on a new branch, we share the secret passphrase, so the clients will always send the MAC code encrypted using this passphrase, and the API will re-hash each request to make sure both results match. This way we're still validating the requests and we'll still remain true to REST, because this method is stateless. We're just simplifying the addition of new client applications.

To explain a bit further, each client will send, on every request, two very specific pieces of information:

- A special header called `hmacdata` with the information being encrypted

- The `api_key` parameter with the value of the encryption result

Upon receiving the request, the API will grab the data from the header and encrypt it again using the correct passphrase. If the result is the same as the value of the `api_key` parameter, then it'll dim the request as authentic. Otherwise, it'll reject the request with a 401 error code.

A Small Backdoor for Swagger

The other change that we're making is because the Swagger UI has no de facto support for our authentication scheme. We can send a fixed `api_key` parameter, but we would have to change the code of the client to get it to use the same algorithm we're using.

This is why we've added a small backdoor in our code, to let the Swagger -UI go by without needing to authenticate each request.

The hack is very simple. Since the UI can send a fixed `api_key`, then we'll let all requests that have an `api_key` equal to 777 pass, automatically trusting them.

This backdoor will need to be removed when going into production to avoid any security issues, of course.

Once this has been added, you can visit `http://localhost:9000/swagger-ui` to check out the UI.

MVC

In Chapter 4, I went over several variations of the MVC pattern, but never actually settled on one to be used on our API. Personally, I really liked the idea behind Hierarchical MVC, since it allows for some really clean code.

That said, it also means extra work when developing, and considering that there aren't many cases where in one controller we're dealing with resources from another, we'll just try to keep it simple and go with a basic MVC.

This means that we'll have the following key elements in our project:

- *Controllers*: Handles requests and calls upon the models for further action

- *Models*: Holds the main logic of the API. Since in our simple case that logic is basically querying the database, these will be the models used by Mongoose. This will simplify our architecture. Also, Mongoose provides different mechanisms to add extra behaviors to our models (things like setting instance methods or post-action hooks).

- *View*: The view will be embedded inside the model's code in the form of a method that translates the specifics of one model into a HAL + JSON that can be returned back to the client.

Folder Structure

To completely understand the design behind our API, let's quickly take a look at the folder structure that I've set up (see Figure 7-1).

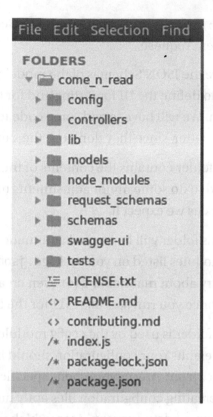

Figure 7-1. *Project folder structure*

Here are the folders we'll be creating and using:

- `controllers`: This folder contains the code for our controllers. It also has an `index.js` file to handle exporting the contents of the required controller files. There is also a base controller here, which contains all the generic methods that all controllers should have; so every new controller can extend this and inherit said methods.

- `lib`: This folder contains the miscellaneous code not big enough to have its own folder but required across several different places in our project; for instance, database access, helper functions, and so forth.

- `models`: Inside this folder are the model files. Normally when working with Mongoose, a model's file has the schema definition, and you return the instantiation of that schema as your model. In our case, the actual definition is somewhere else, so this code handles loading that external definition, adding the extra behavior specific to each model, and then returning it.

- **request_schemas**: Inside this folder are the JSON Schemas used to validate the different requests.

- **schemas**: These are the JSON Schemas of the models, used for the Swagger module to define the UI for testing and for the Mongoose model's definition. We will have to add some code to translate from the first one to the latter, since they don't use the same format.

- **swagger-ui**: This folder contains the contents of the Swagger UI project. We'll need to do some minor adjustments to the index.html file to make it work as we expect it.

- **node_modules**: This folder will be created automatically by npm, and it'll contain the modules listed on you package.json file. You don't really have to worry about maintaining (or even creating) this folder, it'll appear there once you run npm install for the first time.

- **config**: The config folder is used by the config module, which will look inside it by default. Your configuration should be inside a JSON file called default.json. Any environment-specific configuration will be added by creating configuration files aptly named (such as production.json, or development.json, which you can later reference using the NODE_ENV environment variable[1]).

The Source Code

Here I'll list the entire code for the project, including some basic description of the code if required. I'll go folder by folder, following the order shown in Figure 7-1.

The default configuration values are stored in this file (Listing 7-1). This JSON contains values later used throughout the code, as you'll see. You could simply require the file, and directly access those values, but by accessing them through the config modue, you'll get the right behavior when dealing with multiple environment-specific configurations.

---

[1]See the official documentation for more details https://www.npmjs.com/package/config

config

Listing 7-1. config/default.json

```
{
    "secretKey": "this is a secret key, right here",
    "env": "Default",
    "server": {
        "name": "ComeNRead API",
        "version": "2.0.0",
        "port": 9000
    },
    "database": {
        "host": "mongodb://localhost",
        "dbname": "comenread"
    }
}
```

Controllers

This file (Listing 7-2) is used to export each controller. Using this technique, we can import the entire folder like if it was a module, like this:

Listing 7-2. /controllers/index.js

```
module.exports = {
        BookSales: require("./booksales"),
        Stores: require("./stores"),
        Employees: require("./employees"),
        ClientReviews: require("./clientreviews"),
        Clients: require("./clients"),
        Books: require("./books"),
        Authors: require("./authors")
}

var controllers = require("/controllers")
```

Listing 7-3. /controllers/basecontroller.js

```
const restify = require("restify"),
       errors = require("restify-errors"),
       halson = require("halson"),
       logger = require("../lib/logger")

class BaseController {
       constructor() {
              this.actions = []
              this.server = null
       }

       setUpActions(app ,sw) {
              this.server = app
              this.actions.forEach(act => {
                     let method = act['spec']['method']
                     logger.info(`Setting up auto-doc for (${method} ) -
                     ${act['spec']['nickname']}`)
                     sw['add' + method](act)
                     app[method.toLowerCase()](act['spec']['path'],
                     act['action'])
              })
       }

       addAction(spec, fn) {
              let newAct = {
                     'spec': spec,
                     action: fn.bind(this)
              }
              this.actions.push(newAct)
       }

       RESTError(type, msg) {
              logger.error("Error of type" + type + "found:" + msg.
              toString());
```

```
            if(errors[type]) {
                    return new errors[type](msg.toString())
            } else {
                    return {
                            error: true,
                            type: type,
                            msg: msg
                    }
            }
    }

    writeHAL(res, obj) {
            if(Array.isArray(obj)) {
                    let newArr = obj.map( item => {
                            return item.toHAL();
                    })
                    obj = halson(newArr)
            } else {
                    if(obj && obj.toHAL) {
                            obj = obj.toHAL()
                    }
            }
            if(!obj) {
                    obj = {}
            }
            res.json(obj)
    }

}

module.exports = BaseController
```

Every controller extends this class (Listing 7-3), gaining access to the methods shown earlier. We'll use basic prototypical inheritance, as you'll see in a bit when we start listing the other controllers' code.

Let's quickly go over the methods exposed in the code from Listing 7-3.

- `setUpActions`: This method is called upon instantiation of the controller; it is meant to add the actual routes to the HTTP server. This method is called during the initialization sequence for all controllers exported by the `index.js` file.

- `addAction`: This method defines an action, which consists of the specs for that action and the actual function code. The specs are used by Swagger to create the documentation, but they're also used by our code to set up the route; so there are bits inside the JSON spec that are also meant for the server, such as the `path` and `method` attributes.

- `RESTError`: This is a simple wrapper method around all the error methods provided by Restify's error extension.[2] It provides the benefit of cleaner code.

- `writeHAL`: Every model defined (as you'll see soon enough) has a `toHAL` method, and the `writeHAL` methods take care of calling it for every model we're trying to render. It basically centralizes the logic that deals with collections or simple objects, depending on what we're trying to render.

Listing 7-4. /controllers/books.js

```
const BaseController = require("./basecontroller"),
  swagger = require("swagger-node-restify")

class Books extends BaseController {

  constructor(lib) {
    super();
    this.lib = lib;
  }

  /**
  Helper method for the POST action, it takes two lists of items with
  properties calls "store" and "copies" and returns a single list, with
  "store" being a unique key
  */
```

---

[2]See https://github.com/restify/errors.

```
mergeStores(list1, list2) {
  let stores1 = {}
  let stores2 = {}

  let storesMap1 = list1.reduce( (theMap, theItem)  => {
    if(theItem.store) theMap[theItem.store] = theItem.copies;
    return theMap;
  }, {})

  let storesMap2 = list2.reduce( (theMap, theItem)  => {
    if(theItem.store) theMap[theItem.store] = theItem.copies;
    return theMap;
  }, {})

  let stores = Object.assign(storesMap1, storesMap2)
  return Object.keys().map( (k) => {
    return {store: k, copies: stores[k]}
  })
}
list(req, res, next) {
  let criteria = {}
  if(req.params.q) {
    let expr = new RegExp('.*' + req.params.q + '.*')
    criteria.$or = [
      {title: expr},
      {isbn_code: expr},
      {description: expr}
    ]
  }
  if(req.params.genre) {
    criteria.genre = req.params.genre
  }
```

```
  this.lib.db.model('Book')
    .find(criteria)
    .populate('stores.store')
    .exec((err, books) => {
      if(err) return next(err)
      this.writeHAL(res, books)
    })
}

details(req, res, next) {
  let id = req.params.id
  if(id) {
    this.lib.db.model("Book")
      .findOne({_id: id})
      .populate('authors')
      .populate('stores')
      .populate('reviews')
      .exec((err, book) => {
        if(err) return next(this.RESTError('InternalServerError', err))
        if(!book) {
          return next(this.RESTError('ResourceNotFoundError', 'Book not
          found'))
        }
        this.writeHAL(res, book)
      })
  } else {
    next(this.RESTError('InvalidArgumentError', 'Missing book id'))
  }
}

create(req, res, next) {
  let bookData = req.body
  if(bookData) {
    let isbn = bookData.isbn_code
    this.lib.db.model("Book")
      .findOne({isbn_code: isbn})
      .exec((err, bookModel) => {
```

```
        if(!bookModel) {
          bookModel = this.lib.db.model("Book")(bookData)
        } else {
          bookModel.stores = this.mergeStores(bookModel.stores, bookData.
          stores)
        }
        bookModel.save((err, book) => {
          if(err) return next(this.RESTError('InternalServerError',
          err))
          this.writeHAL(res, book)
        })
      })

  } else {
    next(this.RESTError('InvalidArgumentError', 'Missing content of
    book'))
  }
}

bookAuthors(req, res, next) {
  let id = req.params.id
  if(id) {
    this.lib.db.model("Book")
      .findOne({_id: id})
      .populate('authors')
      .exec((err, book) => {
        if(err) return next(this.RESTError('InternalServerError', err))
        if(!book) {
          return next(this.RESTError('ResourceNotFoundError', 'Book not
          found'))
        }
        thihs.writeHAL(res, book.authors)
      })
  } else {
    next(this.RESTError('InvalidArgumentError', 'Missing book id'))
  }
}
```

```
bookReviews(req, res,next) {
  let id = req.params.id
  if(id) {
    this.lib.db.model("Book")
      .findOne({_id: id})
      .populate('reviews')
      .exec((err, book) => {
        if(err) return next(this.RESTError('InternalServerError', err))
        if(!book) {
          return next(this.RESTError('ResourceNotFoundError', 'Book not
          found'))
        }
        this.writeHAL(res, book.reviews)
      })
  } else {
    next(this.RESTError('InvalidArgumentError', 'Missing book id'))
  }
}

update(req, res, next) {
  let data = req.body
  let id = req.params.id
  if(id) {
    this.lib.db.model("Book").findOne({_id: id}).exec((err, book) => {
    if(err) return next(this.RESTError('InternalServerError', err))
      if(!book) return next(this.RESTError('ResourceNotFoundError', 'Book
      not found'))
      book = Object.assign(book, data)
      book.save((err, data) => {
      if(err) return next(this.RESTError('InternalServerError', err))
        this.writeHAL(res, data.toJSON())
      })
    })
  } else {
    next(this.RESTError('InvalidArgumentError', 'Invalid id received'))
  }
```

```
    }
}

module.exports = function(lib) {
  let controller = new Books(lib);

  controller.addAction({
        'path': '/books',
        'method': 'GET',
        'summary': 'Returns the list of books',
        "params": [ swagger.queryParam('q', 'Search term', 'string'),
        swagger.queryParam('genre','Filter by genre', 'string')],
        'responseClass': 'Book',
        'nickname': 'getBooks'
  }, controller.list)

  controller.addAction({
        'path': '/books/{id}',
        'method': 'GET',
        'params': [ swagger.pathParam('id', 'The Id of the book','int') ],
        'summary': 'Returns the full data of a book',
        'responseClass': 'Book',
        'nickname': 'getBook'
     }, controller.details )

  controller.addAction({
        'path': '/books',
        'method': 'POST',
        'params': [ swagger.bodyParam('book', 'JSON representation of the
        new book','string') ],
        'summary': 'Adds a new book into the collectoin',
        'responseClass': 'Book',
        'nickname': 'newBook'
     }, controller.create)

  controller.addAction({
        'path': '/books/{id}/authors',
        'method': 'GET',
```

```
        'params': [ swagger.pathParam('id', 'The Id of the book','int') ],
        'summary': 'Returns the list of authors of one specific book',
        'responseClass': 'Author',
        'nickname': 'getBooksAuthors'
    }, controller.bookAuthors)

  controller.addAction({
        'path': '/books/{id}/reviews',
        'method': 'GET',
        'params': [ swagger.pathParam('id', 'The Id of the book','int') ],
        'summary': 'Returns the list of reviews of one specific book',
        'responseClass': 'BookReview',
        'nickname': 'getBooksReviews'
    }, controller.bookReviews)

  controller.addAction({
        'path': '/books/{id}',
        'method': 'PUT',
        'params': [ swagger.pathParam('id', 'The Id of the book to
        update','string'),
                    swagger.bodyParam('book', 'The data to change on the
                    book', 'string') ],
        'summary': 'Updates the information of one specific book',
        'responseClass': 'Book',
        'nickname': 'updateBook'
    }, controller.update)
  return controller
}
```

The code for this controller (Listing 7-4) is very straightforward; in it we see the basic mechanics we've defined for this particular project, on how to declare a controller and its actions. We also have the special case for the POST action, which takes care of checking for the ISBN of the new book to see if it is trying to add it in stock at another store. If the ISBN already exists, then the book is merged to all the relevant stores (method mergeStores); otherwise, it'll just create the new record.

For every controller, we're creating a new class that inherits from the BaseController, which gives us the ability to add custom behavior if we wanted to and also to remove the common code (such as the setUpActions and RESTError methods) and move it into a single place.

The controller files are required during initialization of the API and then used on the setUpRoutes function inside the helpers.js file. And when that happens, the lib object is passed to them:

```
function setupRoutes(server, swagger, lib) {
        for(controller in lib.controllers) {
                cont = lib.controllers[controller](lib)
                cont.setUpActions(server, swagger)
        }
}
```

This in turn, means that the lib object is received by the export function, which is the one in charge of instantiating the new controller and setting up its actions as part of swagger's documentation to finally return it back to the requiring code.

Here are some other interesting bits from Listing 7-4:

- The getBooks action shows how to do simple regular expression–based filtering with Mongoose.

- The update action is not actually using the update method from Mongoose but instead loads the model using the extend method from the underscore, and finally calls the save method on the model. This is done for one simple reason: the update method doesn't trigger any post-hooks on the models, but the save method does, so if we wanted to add behavior to react to an update on the model, this would be the way to go about it.

Listing 7-5. /controllers/stores.js

```
const BaseController = require("./basecontroller"),
        swagger = require("swagger-node-restify")

class Stores extends BaseController {
```

```
constructor(lib) {
  super();
  this.lib = lib;
}

list(req, res, next) {
  let criteria = {}
  if(req.params.state) {
    criteria.state = new RegExp(req.params.state,'i')
  }
  this.lib.db.model('Store')
    .find(criteria)
    .exec((err, list) =>  {
      if(err) return next(this.RESTError('InternalServerError', err))
      this.writeHAL(res, list)
    })
}

details(req, res, next) {
  let id = req.params.id
  if(id) {
    this.lib.db.model('Store')
      .findOne({_id: id})
      .populate('employees')
      .exec((err, data) => {
      if(err) return next(this.RESTError('InternalServerError', err))
      if(!data) return next(this.RESTError('ResourceNotFoundError',
      'Store not found'))

      this.writeHAL(res, data)
    })
  } else {
    next(this.RESTError('InvalidArgumentError', 'Invalid id'))
  }
}
```

```
storeBooks(req, res, next) {
  let id = req.params.id
  if(id) {

    let criteria = {stores: {$elemMatch: {"store": id}}}
    if(req.params.q) {
      let expr = new RegExp('.*' + req.params.q + '.*', 'i')
      criteria.$or = [
        {title: expr},
        {isbn_code: expr},
        {description: expr}
      ]
    }
    if(req.params.genre) {
      criteria.genre = req.params.genre
    }

    //even though this is the stores controller, we deal directly with
    books here
    this.lib.db.model('Book')
      .find(criteria)
      .populate('authors')
      .exec((err, data) => {
        if(err) return next(this.RESTError('InternalServerError', err))
        this.writeHAL(res, data)
      })
  } else {
    next(this.RESTError('InvalidArgumentError', 'Invalid id'))
  }
}

storeEmployees(req, res, next) {
  let id = req.params.id
  if(id) {
    this.lib.db.model('Store')
      .findOne({_id: id})
```

```
        .populate('employees')
        .exec((err, data) => {
          if(err) return next(this.RESTError('InternalServerError', err))
          if(!data) {
            return next(this.RESTError('ResourceNotFoundError', 'Store not
            found'))
          }
          console.log(data)
          this.writeHAL(res, data.employees)
        })
    } else {
      next(this.RESTError('InvalidArgumentError', 'Invalid id'))
    }
  }

  storeBooksales(req, res, next) {
    let id = req.params.id
    if(id) {
      //even though this is the stores controller, we deal directly with
      booksales here
      this.lib.db.model('Booksale')
        .find({store: id})
        .populate('client')
        .populate('employee')
        .populate('books')
        .exec((err, data) => {
          if(err) return next(this.RESTError('InternalServerError', err))
          this.writeHAL(res, data)
        })
    } else {
      next(this.RESTError('InvalidArgumentError', 'Invalid id'))
    }
  }

  create(req, res, next) {
    let data = req.body
```

```javascript
      if(data) {
        let newStore = this.lib.db.model('Store')(data)
        newStore.save((err, store) => {
          if(err) return next(this.RESTError('InternalServerError', err))
          this.writeHAL(res, store)
        })
      } else {
        next(this.RESTError('InvalidArgumentError', 'No data received'))
      }
    }

    update(req, res, next) {
      let data = req.body
      let id = req.params.id
      if(id) {

        this.lib.db.model("Store").findOne({_id: id}).exec((err, store) => {
        if(err) return next(this.RESTError('InternalServerError', err))
          if(!store) return next(this.RESTError('ResourceNotFoundError',
          'Store not found'))
          store = Object.assign(store, data)
          store.save((err, data) => {
            if(err) return next(this.RESTError('InternalServerError', err))
            this.writeHAL(res, data);
          })
        })
      } else {
        next(this.RESTError('InvalidArgumentError', 'Invalid id received'))
      }
    }
  }

module.exports = lib => {
  let controller = new Stores(lib);

  controller.addAction({
          'path': '/stores',
          'method': 'GET',
```

```
        'summary': 'Returns the list of stores ',
    'params': [swagger.queryParam('state', 'Filter the list of stores by
            state', 'string')],
        'responseClass': 'Store',
        'nickname': 'getStores'
}, controller.list);

controller.addAction({
        'path': '/stores/{id}',
        'method': 'GET',
        'params': [swagger.pathParam('id','The id of the
                store','string')],
        'summary': 'Returns the data of a store',
        'responseClass': 'Store',
        'nickname': 'getStore'
}, controller.details )

controller.addAction({
    'path': '/stores/{id}/books',
    'method': 'GET',
    'params': [swagger.pathParam('id','The id of the store','string'),
            swagger.queryParam('q', 'Search parameter for the books',
            'string'),
            swagger.queryParam('genre', 'Filter results by genre',
            'string')],
    'summary': 'Returns the list of books of a store',
    'responseClass': 'Book',
    'nickname': 'getStoresBooks'
}, controller.storeBooks)

controller.addAction({
        'path': '/stores/{id}/employees',
        'method': 'GET',
        'params': [swagger.pathParam('id','The id of the
                store','string')],
        'summary': 'Returns the list of employees working on a store',
        'responseClass': 'Employee',
```

```
        'nickname': 'getStoresEmployees'
}, controller.storeEmployees)

controller.addAction({
        'path': '/stores/{id}/booksales',
        'method': 'GET',
        'params': [swagger.pathParam('id','The id of the store','string')],
        'summary': 'Returns the list of booksales done on a store',
        'responseClass': 'BookSale',
        'nickname': 'getStoresBookSales'
}, controller.storeBooksales)

controller.addAction({
        'path': '/stores',
        'method': 'POST',
        'summary': 'Adds a new store to the list',
  'params': [swagger.bodyParam('store', 'The JSON data of the store',
  'string')],
        'responseClass': 'Store',
        'nickname': 'newStore'
}, controller.create)

controller.addAction({
        'path': '/stores/{id}',
        'method': 'PUT',
        'summary': "UPDATES a store's information",
        'params': [swagger.pathParam('id','The id of the
                store','string'), swagger.bodyParam('store', 'The new
                information to update', 'string')],
        'responseClass': 'Store',
        'nickname': 'updateStore'
}, controller.update)

return controller
}
```

The code from Listing 7-5 is very similar to that of the Books controller. It does, however, have something of notice: the getStoresBookSales action clearly shows what happens when we don't use a Hierarchical MVC model. I said that this is not a common case, so it would be fine for the purpose of this book, but it clearly shows how separation of concerns is broken in the strictest of senses, by acting over the model of another controller instead of going through that other controller. Given the added complexity that mechanism would imply to our code, we're better off looking the other way for the time being.

Listings 7-6 to 7-10 show the code of the three remaining controllers. They don't particularly show anything new compared to the previous ones, so we'll just look at their code and the occasional code comment.

Listing 7-6. /controllers/authors.js

```
const BaseController = require("./basecontroller"),
  swagger = require("swagger-node-restify")

class  BookSales extends BaseController {

  constructor(lib) {
    super();
    this.lib = lib;
  }

  queryAuthors(res, next, criteria, bookIds) {
    if(bookIds) {
      criteria.books = {$in: bookIds}
    }

    this.lib.db.model('Author')
      .find(criteria)
      .exec((err, authors) =>  {
        if(err) return next(this.RESTError('InternalServerError', err))
        this.writeHAL(res, authors)
      })
  }
```

```
list(req, res, next) {
  let criteria = {}
  if(req.params.q) {
    let expr = new RegExp('.*' + req.params.q + '.*', 'i')
    criteria.$or = [
      {name: expr},
      {description: expr}
    ]
  }
  let filterByGenre = false || req.params.genre

  if(filterByGenre) {
    this.lib.logger.debug("Filtering by genre:" + filterByGenre)
    this.lib.db.model('Book')
      .find({genre: filterByGenre})
      .exec((err, books) => {
        if(err) return next(this.RESTError('InternalServerError', err))
        this.queryAuthors(res, next, criteria, _.pluck(books, '_id'))
      })
  } else {
    this.queryAuthors(res, next, criteria)
  }
}

details(req, res, next) {
  let id = req.params.id

  if(id) {
    this.lib.db.model('Author')
      .findOne({_id: id})
      .exec((err, author) => {
        if(err) return next(this.RESTError('InternalServerError', err))
        if(!author) {
          return next(this.RESTError('ResourceNotFoundError', 'Author not
          found'))
        }
```

```
        this.writeHAL(res, author)
      })
  } else {
    next(this.RESTError('InvalidArgumentError', 'Missing author id'))
  }
}

create(req, res, next) {
  let body = req.body

  if(body) {
    let newAuthor = this.lib.db.model('Author')(body)
    newAuthor.save((err, author) => {
      if(err) return next(this.RESTError('InternalServerError', err))
      this.writeHAL(res, author)
    })
  } else {
    next(this.RESTError('InvalidArgumentError', 'Missing author id'))
  }
}

update(req, res, next) {
  let data = req.body
  let id = req.params.id
  if(id) {

    this.lib.db.model("Author").findOne({_id: id}).exec((err, author) =>
{

    if(err) return next(this.RESTError('InternalServerError', err))
        if(!author) return next(this.RESTError('ResourceNotFoundError',
        'Author not found'))
        author = Object.assign(author, data)
        author.save((err, data) => {
          if(err) return next(this.RESTError('InternalServerError', err))
          this.writeHAL(res, data)
        })
      })
```

```
    } else {
      next(this.RESTError('InvalidArgumentError', 'Invalid id received'))
    }
  }

  authorBooks(req, res, next) {
    let id = req.params.id

    if(id) {
      this.lib.db.model('Author')
        .findOne({_id: id})
        .populate('books')
        .exec((err, author) => {
          if(err) return next(this.RESTError('InternalServerError', err))
          if(!author) {
            return next(this.RESTError('ResourceNotFoundError', 'Author not
             found'))
          }
          this.writeHAL(res, author.books)
        })
    } else {
      next(this.RESTError('InvalidArgumentError', 'Missing author id'))
    }
  }
}

module.exports = function(lib) {
  let controller = new BookSales(lib)

  //list
  controller.addAction({
          'path': '/authors',
          'method': 'GET',
          'summary' :'Returns the list of authors across all stores',
          'params': [ swagger.queryParam('genre', 'Filter authors by genre
                    of their books', 'string'),
```

```
                                    swagger.queryParam('q', 'Search
                                    parameter', 'string')],
        'responseClass': 'Author',
        'nickname': 'getAuthors'
}, controller.list)
//get
controller.addAction({
        'path': '/authors/{id}',
        'summary': 'Returns all the data from one specific author',
        'method': 'GET',
    'params': [swagger.pathParam('id','The id of the author','string')],
        'responseClass': 'Author',
        'nickname': 'getAuthor'
}, controller.details )

//post

controller.addAction({
        'path': '/authors',
        'summary': 'Adds a new author to the database',
        'method': 'POST',
        'params': [swagger.bodyParam('author', 'JSON representation of
                    the data', 'string')],
        'responseClass': 'Author',
        'nickname': 'addAuthor'
}, controller.create )

//put

controller.addAction({
        'path': '/authors/{id}',
        'method': 'PUT',
        'summary': "UPDATES an author's information",
        'params': [swagger.pathParam('id','The id of the author','string'),
                            swagger.bodyParam('author', 'The new
                            information to update', 'string')],
```

```
            'responseClass': 'Author',
            'nickname': 'updateAuthor'
    }, controller.update)

    // /books
    controller.addAction({
            'path': '/authors/{id}/books',
            'summary': 'Returns the data from all the books of one specific
                    author',
            'method': 'GET',
            'params': [ swagger.pathParam('id', 'The id of the author',
                    'string')],
            'responseClass': 'Book',
            'nickname': 'getAuthorsBooks'
    }, controller.authorBooks )

    return controller
}
```

Listing 7-7. /controllers/booksales.js

```
const BaseController = require("./basecontroller"),
  swagger = require("swagger-node-restify")

class BookSales extends BaseController {

  constructor(lib) {
    super();
    this.lib = lib;
  }

  list(req, res, next) {

    let criteria = {}
    if(req.params.start_date)
      criteria.date = {$gte: req.params.start_date}
    if(req.params.end_date)
      criteria.date = {$lte: req.params.end_date}
```

```
    if(req.params.store_id)
      criteria.store = req.params.store_id

    this.lib.db.model("Booksale")
      .find(criteria)
      .populate('books')
      .populate('client')
      .populate('employee')
      .populate('store')
      .exec((err, sales) => {
        if(err) return next(this.RESTError('InternalServerError', err))
        this.writeHAL(res, sales)
      })
  }

  create(req, res, next) {
    let body = req.body
    if(body) {
      let newSale = this.lib.db.model("Booksale")(body)
      newSale.save((err, sale) => {
        if(err) return next(ths.RESTError('InternalServerError', err))
        this.writeHAL(res, sale)
      })
    } else {
      next(this.RESTError('InvalidArgumentError', 'Missing json data'))
    }
  }
}

module.exports = function(lib) {
  let controller = new BookSales(lib);

  controller.addAction({
        'path': '/booksales',
        'method': 'GET',
        'summary': 'Returns the list of book sales',
```

```
        'params': [ swagger.queryParam('start_date', 'Filter sales done
                after (or on) this date', 'string'),
                swagger.queryParam('end_date', 'Filter sales done on or
                before this date', 'string'),
                swagger.queryParam('store_id', 'Filter sales done  on
                this store', 'string')
                ],
        'responseClass': 'BookSale',
        'nickname': 'getBookSales'
    }, controller.list)

  controller.addAction({
        'path': '/booksales',
        'method': 'POST',
        'params': [ swagger.bodyParam('booksale', 'JSON representation of
                the new booksale','string') ],
        'summary': 'Records a new booksale',
        'responseClass': 'BookSale',
        'nickname': 'newBookSale'
    }, controller.create)

  return controller
}
```

Listing 7-8. /controllers/clientreviews.js

```
const BaseController = require("./basecontroller"),
        swagger = require("swagger-node-restify")

class ClientReviews extends BaseController {

  constructor(lib) {
    super();
    this.lib = lib;
  }
```

```
  create(req, res, next) {
    let body = req.body
    if(body) {

      let newReview = this.lib.db.model('ClientReview')(body)
      newReview.save((err, rev) => {
        if(err) return next(this.RESTError('InternalServerError', err))
        this.writeHAL(res, rev)
      })
    }
  }
}

module.exports = function(lib) {
  let controller = new ClientReviews(lib);

  controller.addAction({
          'path': '/clientreviews',
          'method': 'POST',
          'summary': 'Adds a new client review to a book',
          'params': [swagger.bodyParam('review', 'The JSON representation
                  of the review',  'string')],
          'responseClass': 'ClientReview',
          'nickname': 'addClientReview'
  }, controller.create)

  return controller
}
```

Listing 7-9. /controllers/clients.js

```
const BaseController = require("./basecontroller"),
        swagger = require("swagger-node-restify")

class Clients extends BaseController {

  constructor(lib) {
   super();
   this.lib = lib;
  }
```

```
  list(req, res, next) {
    this.lib.db.model('Client').find().sort('name').exec((err, clients) =>
{
      if(err) return next(this.RESTError('InternalServerError', err))
      this.writeHAL(res, clients)
    })
  }

  create(req, res, next) {
    let newClient = req.body

    let newClientModel = this.lib.db.model('Client')(newClient)
    newClientModel.save((err, client) => {
      if(err) return next(this.RESTError('InternalServerError', err))
      this.writeHAL(res, client)
    })
  }

  details(req, res, next) {
    let id = req.params.id
    if(id != null) {
      this.lib.db.model('Client').findOne({_id: id}).exec((err, client) =>
{
        if(err) return next(this.RESTError('InternalServerError',err))
        if(!client) return next(this.RESTError('ResourceNotFoundError',
        'The client id cannot be found'))
        this.writeHAL(res, client)
      })
    } else {
      next(this.RESTError('InvalidArgumentError','Invalid client id'))
    }
  }

  update(req, res, next) {
    let id = req.params.id
    if(!id) {
      return next(this.RESTError('InvalidArgumentError','Invalid id'))
    } else {
```

```javascript
      let model = this.lib.db.model('Client')
      model.findOne({_id: id})
        .exec((err, client) => {
          if(err) return next(this.RESTError('InternalServerError', err))
          client = Object.assign(client, req.body)
          client.save((err, newClient) => {
            if(err) return next(this.RESTError('InternalServerError', err))
            this.writeHAL(res, newClient)
          })
        })
    }

  }
}
module.exports = (lib) => {
  let controller = new Clients(lib);

  controller.addAction({
          'path': '/clients',
          'method': 'GET',
          'summary': 'Returns the list of clients ordered by name',
          'responseClass':'Client',
          'nickname': 'getClients'
  }, controller.list )

  controller.addAction({
          'path': '/clients',
          'method': 'POST',
          'params': [swagger.bodyParam('client', 'The JSON representation
                  of the client', 'string')],
          'summary': 'Adds a new client to the database',
          'responseClass': 'Client',
          'nickname': 'addClient'
  }, controller.create )

  controller.addAction({
          'path': '/clients/{id}',
          'method': 'GET',
```

```
        'params': [swagger.pathParam('id', 'The id of the client',
                'string')],
        'summary': 'Returns the data of one client',
        'responseClass': 'Client',
        'nickname': 'getClient'
}, controller.details)

controller.addAction({
        'path': '/clients/{id}',
        'method': 'PUT',
        'params': [swagger.pathParam('id', 'The id of the client',
                'string'), swagger.bodyParam('client', 'The content to
                overwrite', 'string')],
        'summary': 'Updates the data of one client',
        'responseClass': 'Client',
        'nickname': 'updateClient'
}, controller.update )

    return controller
}
```

Listing 7-10. /controllers/employees.js

```
const BaseController = require("./basecontroller"),
        swagger = require("swagger-node-restify")

class Employees extends BaseController {
  constructor(lib) {
    super();
    this.lib = lib;
  }

  list(req, res, next) {
    this.lib.db.model('Employee').find().exec((err, list) => {
      if(err) return next(this.RESTError('InternalServerError', err))
      this.writeHAL(res, list)
    })
  }
```

```
details(req, res, next) {
  let id = req.params.id
  if(id) {
    this.lib.db.model('Employee').findOne({_id: id}).exec((err, empl) => {
      if(err) return next(err)
      if(!empl) {
        return next(this.RESTError('ResourceNotFoundError', 'Not found'))
      }
      this.writeHAL(res, empl)
    })
  } else {
    next(this.RESTError('InvalidArgumentError', 'Invalid id'))
  }
}

create(req, res, next) {
  let data = req.body
  if(data) {
    let newEmployee = this.lib.db.model('Employee')(data)
    console.log(newEmployee)
    newEmployee.save((err, emp) => {
      if(err) return next(this.RESTError('InternalServerError', err))
      this.writeHAL(res, emp)
    })
  } else {
    next(this.RESTError('InvalidArgumentError', 'No data received'))
  }
}

update(req, res, next) {
  let data = req.body
  let id = req.params.id
  if(id) {

    this.lib.db.model("Employee").findOne({_id: id}).exec((err, emp) => {
      if(err) return next(this.RESTError('InternalServerError', err))
      emp = Object.assign(emp, data)
```

```
      emp.save((err, employee) => {
        if(err) return next(this.RESTError('InternalServerError', err))
        this.writeHAL(res, employee)
      })
    })
  } else {
    next(this.RESTError('InvalidArgumentError','Invalid id received'))
  }
 }
}

module.exports = function(lib) {
  let controller = new Employees(lib);

  controller.addAction({
          'path': '/employees',
          'method': 'GET',
          'summary': 'Returns the list of employees across all stores',
          'responseClass': 'Employee',
          'nickname': 'getEmployees'
  }, controller.list)

  controller.addAction({
          'path': '/employees/{id}',
          'method': 'GET',
          'params': [swagger.pathParam('id','The id of the
                     employee','string')],
          'summary': 'Returns the data of an employee',
          'responseClass': 'Employee',
          'nickname': 'getEmployee'
  }, controller.details)

  controller.addAction({
          'path': '/employees',
          'method': 'POST',
          'params': [swagger.bodyParam('employee', 'The JSON data of the
                     employee', 'string')],
```

```
        'summary': 'Adds a new employee to the list',
        'responseClass': 'Employee',
        'nickname': 'newEmployee'
}, controller.create)

controller.addAction({
        'path': '/employees/{id}',
        'method': 'PUT',
        'summary': "UPDATES an employee's information",
        'params': [swagger.pathParam('id','The id of the
                employee','string'), swagger.bodyParam('employee',
                'The new information to update', 'string')],
        'responseClass': 'Employee',
        'nickname': 'updateEmployee'
}, controller.update)

return controller
}
```

lib

As mentioned, the lib folder contains all sorts of helper functions and utilities that were just too small to be put into a separate folder, but important and generic enough to be used in several places of the code.

/lib/index.js

Listing 7-11. Code for the Main lib File, which Provides Access to the Exported Modules

```
const mongoose = require("mongoose");

module.exports = {
        helpers: require("./helpers"),
        logger: require("./logger"),
        controllers: require("../controllers"),
        schemas: require("../schemas"),
```

```
        schemaValidator: require("./schemaValidator"),
        db: require("./db")(mongoose)
}
```

This file is meant to act as the single point of contact between the outside world (the rest of the project) and the inside world (all of the mini-modules grouped within this folder). There is nothing special about it. This file is simply used as a centralizer for all the require statements you'd use throughout your code if you were to individually require the specific files. In other words, it just does a require for everything and exports the returned code using predefined keys.

Listing 7-12. /lib/helpers.js

```
const halson = require("halson"),
      config = require("config");

module.exports = {
        makeHAL: makeHAL,
        setupRoutes: setupRoutes,
        validateKey: validateKey
}

function setupRoutes(server, swagger, lib) {
        for(controller in lib.controllers) {
                cont = lib.controllers[controller](lib)
                cont.setUpActions(server, swagger)
        }
}

/**
Makes sure to sign every request and compare it
against the key sent by the client, this way
we make sure it's authentic

*/
function validateKey(hmacdata, key, lib) {
        //This is for testing the swagger-ui, should be removed after
        development to avoid possible security problem :)
```

```
        if(+key == 777) return true
        let hmac = require("crypto").createHmac("md5", config.
        get('secretKey'))
            .update(hmacdata)
            .digest("hex");
        return hmac == key
}

function makeHAL(data, links, embed) {
        let obj = halson(data)

        if(links && links.length > 0) {
                links.forEach( lnk => {
                        obj.addLink(lnk.name, {
                                href: lnk.href,
                                title: lnk.title || ''
                        })
                })
        }

        if(embed && embed.length > 0) {
                embed.forEach( item => {
                        obj.addEmbed(item.name, item.data)
                })
        }

        return obj
}
```

Just as the modules exported by the index.js file are too small to merit their own folder, these functions (Listing 7-12) are too small and particular to merit their own module, so instead they are grouped here, inside the helpers module. The functions are meant to be of use (hence, the name "helpers") throughout the entire project.

Let's quickly go over each of these names:

> setupRoutes: This function is called from within the project's main file during boot-up time. It's meant to initialize all controllers, which in turn adds the actual route's code to the HTTP server.

validateKey: This function contains the code to validate the request by recalculating the HMAC key. And as mentioned earlier, it contains the exception to the rule, allowing any request to validate if the key sent is 777.

makeHAL: This function turns any type of object into a HAL JSON object ready to be rendered. This particular function is heavily used from within the models' code.

Listing 7-13. /lib/schemaValidator.js

```
const tv4 = require("tv4"),
      formats = require("tv4-formats"),
      schemas = require("../request_schemas/")

module.exports = {
      validateRequest: validate
}

function validate (req) {
      let res = {valid: true}
      tv4.addFormat(formats)
      let schemaKey = req.route ? req.route.path.toString().
      replace("/", "") : ''
      let actionKey = req.route.name
      let mySchema = null,
            myData = null;
      if(schemas[schemaKey]){
            mySchema = schemas[schemaKey][actionKey]
            data = null
            if(mySchema) {
                  switch(mySchema.validate) {
                        case 'params':
                              data = req.params
                        break
                  }
```

```
                        res = tv4.validateMultiple(data, mySchema.schema)
                }
        }

      return res
}
```

This file (Listing 7-13) has the code that validates any request against a JSON Schema that we define. The only function of interest is the `validate` function, which validates the request object. It also counts on a predefined structure inside the request, which is added by Swagger (the `route` attribute).

As you might've guessed from Listing 7-13 code, the validation of a request is optional; not every request is being validated. And right now, only query parameters are validated, but this can be extended by simply adding a new case to the switch statement.

This function works with the premise of "convention over configuration," which means that if you set up everything "right," then you don't have to do much. In our particular case, we're looking inside the `request_schemas` folder to load a set of predefined schemas, which have a very specific format. In that format we find the name of the action (the nickname that we set up) to validate and the portion of the request we want to validate. In our particular function, we're only validating query parameters for things such as invalid formats and so forth. The only request we have set up to validate right now is the BookSales listing action; but if we wanted to add a new validation, it would just be a matter of adding a new schema—no programming required.

Listing 7-14. /lib/db.js

```
const config = require("config"),
      _ = require("underscore"),
      mongoose = require("mongoose"),

      Schema = mongoose.Schema

let obj = {
      cachedModels: {},
      getModelFromSchema: getModelFromSchema,
      model: function(mname) {
              return this.models[mname]
      },
```

```
        connect: function(cb) {
                mongoose.connect(config.database.host + "/" + config.
                database.dbname)
                this.connection = mongoose.connection
                this.connection.on('error', cb)
                this.connection.on('open', cb)
        }
}

obj.models = require("../models/")(obj)

module.exports = obj

function translateComplexType(v, strType) {
        let tmp = null
        let type = strType || v['type']
        switch(type) {
                case 'array':
                        tmp = []
                        if(v['items']['$ref'] != null) {
                                tmp.push({
                                        type: Schema.ObjectId,
                                        ref: v['items']['$ref']
                                })
                        } else {
                                let originalType = v['items']['type']
                                v['items']['type'] =
                                translateTypeToJs(v['items']['type'])
                                tmp.push(translateComplexType(v['items'],
                                originalType))
                        }
                break;
                case 'object':
                        tmp = {}
                        let props = v['properties']
                        _.each(props, (data, k) => {
```

```
                                        if(data['$ref'] != null) {
                                            tmp[k] = {
                                                    type: Schema.ObjectId,
                                                    ref: data['$ref']
                                            }
                                        } else {
                                            tmp[k] = translateTypeToJs
                                            (data['type'])
                                        }
                            })
                break;
                default:
                        tmp = v
                        tmp['type'] = translateTypeToJs(type)
                break;
        }
        return tmp
}

/**
Turns the JSON Schema into a Mongoose schema
*/
function getModelFromSchema(schema) {
        let data = {
                name: schema.id,
                schema: {}
        }

        let newSchema = {}
        let tmp = null
        _.each(schema.properties, (v, propName) => {
                if(v['$ref'] != null) {
                        tmp = {
                                type: Schema.Types.ObjectId,
                                ref: v['$ref']
                        }
                } else {
```

```
                        tmp = translateComplexType(v) //{}
            }
            newSchema[propName] = tmp
    })

    data.schema = new Schema(newSchema)
    return data
}

function translateTypeToJs(t) {
    if(t.indexOf('int') === 0) {
        t = "number"
    }
    return eval(t.charAt(0).toUpperCase() + t.substr(1))
}
```

Listing 7-14 contains some interesting functions that are used a lot from the models'
code. In Chapter 5 I mentioned that the schemas used with Swagger could potentially
be reused to do other things, such as defining the models' schemas. But to do this, we
need a function to translate the standard JSON Schema into the nonstandard JSON
format required by Mongoose to define a model. This is where the getModelFromSchema
function comes into play; its code is meant to go over the structure of the JSON Schema
and create a new, simpler JSON structure to be used as a Mongoose Schema.

The other functions are more straightforward:

- *connect:* Connects to the database server and sets up the callbacks for
  both error and success cases

- *model:* Accesses the model from outside. We could just directly
  access the models using the object *models,* but it's always a good idea
  to provide a wrapper in case you ever need to add extra behaviors
  (such as checking for errors).

Finally, as seen in Listing 7-15, the main logging function is defined in this file.
Thanks to the module Winston[3] (which you can add by doing npm install winston
--save) we're able to define a generic and powerful logger, with a standard output
format for all messages and the possibility of adding the "transports" if needed.

---

[3]See https://www.npmjs.com/package/winston

Listing 7-15. /lib/logger.js

```javascript
const config = require("config");

let _ENV = process.env.NODE_ENV || config.get('env');

const { createLogger, format, addColors, transports } = require('winston');
const { combine, timestamp, label, printf, colorize } = format;

const myFormat = printf(info => {
  return `${info.timestamp} [${info.label}] ${info.level}: ${info.message}`;
});

const myCustomLevels = {
  levels: {
    error: 0,
    warn: 1,
    info: 2,
    debug: 3,
  },
  colors: {
    error: 'red',
    warn: 'yellow',
    info: 'blue',
    debug: 'violet'
  }
};

const logger = createLogger({
  format: combine(
    colorize(),
    label({ label: _ENV }),
    timestamp(),
    myFormat
  ),
  levels: myCustomLevels.levels,
  transports: [new transports.Console()]
});
```

```
addColors(myCustomLevels)

module.exports = logger;
```

By default, the code assumes the environment set on the default configuration file. This value can be overridden by setting a value for the environment variable NODE_ENV.

Models

This folder contains the actual code of each model. The definition of these resources won't be found in these files because they're only meant to define behavior. The actual properties are defined in the schemas folder (which, again, is being used both by the models and Swagger).

Listing 7-16. /models/index.js

```
module.exports = function(db) {
        return {
                "Book": require("./book")(db),
                "Booksale": require("./booksale")(db),
                "ClientReview": require("./clientreview")(db),
                "Client": require("./client")(db),
                "Employee": require("./employee")(db),
                "Store": require("./store")(db),
                "Author": require("./author")(db)
        }
}
```

Again, as in the other folders, the index.js file (seen in Listing 7-16) allows us to require every model at once and treat this folder like a module itself. The other thing of note here is the passing of the db object to every model, so that they can access the getModelFromSchema function.

Listing 7-17. /models/author.js

```
const mongoose = require("mongoose")
        jsonSelect = require('mongoose-json-select'),
        helpers = require("../lib/helpers");
```

```
module.exports = function(db) {
        let schema = require("../schemas/author.js")
        let modelDef = db.getModelFromSchema(schema)

        modelDef.schema.plugin(jsonSelect, '-books')
        modelDef.schema.methods.toHAL = function() {
                let halObj = helpers.makeHAL(this.toJSON(),
                                                        [{name: 'books',
'href': '/authors/' + this.id + '/books', 'title': 'Books'}])

                if(this.books.length > 0) {
                        if(this.books[0].toString().length != 24) {
                                halObj.addEmbed('books', this.books.map
                                (e => { return e.toHAL() }))

                        }
                }

                return halObj
        }

        return mongoose.model(modelDef.name, modelDef.schema)
}
```

Listing 7-17 shows the basic mechanics of loading the JSON Schema, transforming it into a Mongoose Schema, defining the custom behavior, and finally returning a new model.

The following defines the main custom behaviors:

- The jsonSelect model allows us to define the attributes to add to or remove from the object when turning it into a JSON. We want to remove the embedded objects from the JSON representation, because they will be added to the HAL JSON representation as embedded objects, rather than being part of the main object.

- The toHAL method takes care of returning the representation of the resource in HAL JSON format.

- The links associated to the main object are defined manually. We could improve this by further customizing the code for the loading and transformation of the JSON Schemas of the models.

Note   Checks like the following (inside the `toHAL` method) are meant to determine if the model has populated a reference, or if it is simply the id of the referenced object:

```
if(this.books[0].toString().length != 24) {
  //...
}
```

The following is the rest of the code inside the *models* folder; as you can appreciate, the same mechanics are duplicated on every case.

Listing 7-18. /models/book.js

```
const mongoose = require("mongoose"),
        jsonSelect = require('mongoose-json-select'),
        helpers = require("../lib/helpers")

module.exports = function(db) {
        let schema = require("../schemas/book.js")
        let modelDef = db.getModelFromSchema(schema)

        modelDef.schema.plugin(jsonSelect, '-stores -authors')
        modelDef.schema.methods.toHAL = function() {
                let halObj = helpers.makeHAL(this.toJSON(),
                                        [{name: 'reviews',
                                        href: '/books/' + this.
                                        id + '/reviews', title:
                                        'Reviews'}])

                if(this.stores.length > 0) {
                        if(this.stores[0].store.toString().length != 24) {
                                halObj.addEmbed('stores', this.stores.
                                map(s => { return { store: s.store.toHAL(),
                                copies: s.copies } } ))
                        }
                }
        }
```

```
                    if(this.authors.length > 0) {
                         if(this.authors[0].toString().length != 24) {
                              halObj.addEmbed('authors', this.authors)
                         }
                    }

                    return halObj
          }

          return mongoose.model(modelDef.name, modelDef.schema)
}
```

Listing 7-19. /models/booksale.js

```
const mongoose = require("mongoose"),
          jsonSelect = require('mongoose-json-select'),
          helpers = require("../lib/helpers");

module.exports = db => {
          let schema = require("../schemas/booksale.js")
          let modelDef = db.getModelFromSchema(schema)

          modelDef.schema.plugin(jsonSelect, '-store -employee -client
          -books')
          modelDef.schema.methods.toHAL = function() {
                    let halObj = helpers.makeHAL(this.toJSON());

                    ['books', 'store', 'employee', 'client']
                         .filter( prop => {
                              if(Array.isArray(this[prop])) return
                              this[prop][0].toString().length != 24;
                              return this[prop].toString().length != 24
                         })
                         .map( prop => {
                              if(Array.isArray(this[prop])) halObj.
                              addEmbed(prop, this[prop].map(p => { return
                              p.toHAL()}))
```

```
                                else halObj.addEmbed(prop, this[prop].
                                toHAL())
                        })

                return halObj
        }

        return mongoose.model(modelDef.name, modelDef.schema)
}
```

Listing 7-20. /models/client.js

```
const mongoose = require("mongoose"),
        jsonSelect = require('mongoose-json-select'),
        helpers = require("../lib/helpers");

module.exports = db => {
        let schema = require("../schemas/client.js")
        let modelDef = db.getModelFromSchema(schema)

        modelDef.schema.methods.toHAL = function() {
                return helpers.makeHAL(this.toJSON())
        }

        return mongoose.model(modelDef.name, modelDef.schema)
}
```

Listing 7-21. /models/clientreview.js

```
const mongoose = require("mongoose"),
        jsonSelect = require('mongoose-json-select'),
        helpers = require("../lib/helpers");

module.exports = db => {
        let schema = require("../schemas/clientreview.js")
        let modelDef = db.getModelFromSchema(schema)

        modelDef.schema.methods.toHAL = function() {
                return helpers.makeHAL(this.toJSON())
        }
```

```
        modelDef.schema.post('save', function(doc, next) {
                db.model('Book').update({_id: doc.book}, {$addToSet:
                {reviews: this.id}}, next)
        })

        return mongoose.model(modelDef.name, modelDef.schema)
}
```

Listing 7-22. /models/employee.js

```
const mongoose = require("mongoose"),
        jsonSelect = require('mongoose-json-select'),
        helpers = require("../lib/helpers");

module.exports = db => {
        let schema = require("../schemas/employee.js")
        let modelDef = db.getModelFromSchema(schema)

        modelDef.schema.methods.toHAL = function() {
                let json = JSON.stringify(this) //toJSON()
                return helpers.makeHAL(json);
        }

        return mongoose.model(modelDef.name, modelDef.schema)
}
```

Listing 7-23. /models/store.js

```
const mongoose = require("mongoose"),
        jsonSelect = require("mongoose-json-select"),
        helpers = require("../lib/helpers")

module.exports = db => {
        let schema = require("../schemas/store.js")
        let modelDef = db.getModelFromSchema(schema)

        modelDef.schema.plugin(jsonSelect, '-employees')
        modelDef.schema.methods.toHAL = function() {
                let halObj = helpers.makeHAL(this.toJSON(),
```

```
                                     [{name: 'books', href: '/
                                     stores/' + this.id + '/
                                     books', title: 'Books'},
                                     {name: 'employees',
                                     href: '/stores/' + this.
                                     id + '/employees', title:
                                     'Employees'},
                                 {name: 'booksales', href: '/
                                 stores/' + this.id + '/booksales',
                                 title: 'Book Sales'}])
        if(this.employees.length > 0) {
                if(this.employees[0].toString().length != 24) {
                        halObj.addEmbed('employees', this.
                        employees.map(e => { return e.toHAL() }))
                }
        }
        return halObj
    }

    return mongoose.model(modelDef.name, modelDef.schema);
}
```

request_schemas

This folder contains the JSON Schemas that will be used to validate the requests. They need to describe an object and its properties. We should be able to validate against the request object attribute that contains the parameters (normally request.params, but potentially something else, such as request.body).

Due to the type of attributes we defined for our endpoints, there is really only one endpoint that we would want to validate: the getBookSales (GET /booksales) endpoint. It receives two date parameters, and we probably want to validate their format to be 100% certain that the dates are valid.

Again, to provide the simplicity of usage that "convention over configuration" provides, our schema files must follow a very specific format, which is then used by the validator that we saw earlier (see Listing 7-13).

Listing 7-24. Template Code for a Validator

```
/request_schemas/[CONTROLLER NAME].js
module.exports = {
 [ENDPOINT NICKNAME]: {
   validate: [TYPE],
   schema: [JSON SCHEMA]
 }
}
```

There are several pieces that need to be explained in the preceding code:

- CONTROLLER NAME: This means that the file for the schema needs to have the same name as the controller, all lowercase. And since we already did that for our controllers' files, this means the schemas for each controller will have to have the same name as each controller's file.

- ENDPOINT NICKNAME: This should be the nickname given to the action when adding it to the controller (using the addAction method).

- TYPE: The type of object to validate. The only value supported right now is params, which references the query and path parameters received. This could be extended to support other objects.

- JSON SCHEMA: This is where we add the actual JSON Schema defining the request parameters.

Listing 7-25 shows the actual code defining the validation for the getBookSales action.

Listing 7-25. /request_schemas/booksales.js

```
module.exports = {

 getbooksales: {
   validate: 'params',
   schema: {
```

```
    type: "object",
    properties: {
      start_date: {
        type: 'string',
        format:'date'
      },
      end_date: {
        type: 'string',
        format:'date'
      },
      store_id: {
        type: 'string'
      }
    }
  }
}
```

schemas

This folder contains the JSON Schema definitions of our resources, which also translate into the Mongoose Schemas when initializing our models.

The level of detail provided in these files is very important, because it also translates into the actual Mongoose model. This means that we could define things such as ranges of values and format patterns, which would be validated by Mongoose when creating the new resources.

For instance, let's take a look at ClientReview, a schema that makes use of such capability.

Listing 7-26. /schemas/clientreview.js

```
module.exports = {
      "id": "ClientReview",
      "properties": {
              "client": {
```

```
                "$ref": "Client",
                "description": "The client who submits the review"
        },
        "book": {
                "$ref": "Book",
                "description": "The book being reviewed"
        },
        "review_text": {
                "type": "string",
                "description": "The actual review text"
        },
        "stars": {
                "type": "integer",
                "description": "The number of stars, from 0 to 5",
                "min": 0,
                "max": 5
        }
    }
}
```

The stars attribute is clearly setting the maximum and minimum values that we can send when saving a new review. If we tried to send an invalid number, then we would get an error like the one shown in Figure 7-2.

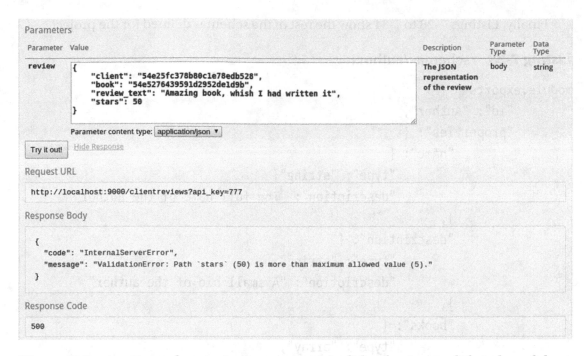

Figure 7-2. *An error when trying to save an invalid value in a validated model*

When defining schemas that reference others, remember to correctly name the reference (the name of each schema is given by the id property). So if you correctly set up the reference, the getModelFromSchema method of the db module will also properly set up the reference in Mongoose (this works both for direct reference and for collections).

Listing 7-27 shows the main file for this folder; the index.js works like the index files in the other folders.

Listing 7-27. schemas/index.js

```
module.exports = {
       models: {
                BookSale: require("./booksale"),
                Book: require("./book"),
                Author: require("./author"),
                Store: require("./store"),
                Employee: require("./employee"),
                Client: require("./client"),
                ClientReview: require("./clientreview")
        }
}
```

Finally, Listings 7-28 to 7-34 show the rest of the schemas defined for the project.

Listing 7-28. /schemas/author.js

```javascript
module.exports = {
        "id": "Author",
        "properties": {
                "name": {
                        "type": "string",
                        "description": "The full name of the author"
                },
                "description": {
                        "type": "string",
                        "description": "A small bio of the author"
                },
                "books": {
                        "type": "array",
                        "description": "The list of books published on at
                                        least one of the stores by this author",
                        "items": {
                                "$ref": "Book"
                        }
                },
                "website": {
                        "type": "string",
                        "description": "The Website url of the author"
                },
                "avatar": {
                        "type": "string",
                        "description": "The url for the avatar of this
                        author"
                }
        }
}
```

Listing 7-29. /schemas/book.js

```javascript
module.exports = {
        "id": "Book",
        "properties": {
                "title": {
                        "type": "string",
                        "description": "The title of the book"
                },
                "authors": {
                        "type":"array",
                        "description":"List of authors of the book",
                        "items": {
                                "$ref": "Author"
                        }
                },
                "isbn_code": {
                        "description": "Unique identifier code of the
                                        book",
                        "type":"string"
                },
                "stores": {
                        "type": "array",
                        "description": "The stores where clients can buy
                                        this book",
                        "items": {
                                "type": "object",
                                "properties": {
                                        "store": {
                                                "$ref": "Store",
                                        },
                                        "copies": {
                                                "type": "integer"
                                        }
                                }
```

```
                    }
            },
            "genre": {
                    "type": "string",
                    "description": "Genre of the book"
            },
            "description": {
                    "type": "string",
                    "description": "Description of the book"
            },
            "reviews": {
                    "type": "array",
                    "items": {
                            "$ref": "ClientReview"
                    }
            },
            "price": {
                    "type": "number",
                    "minimun": 0,
                    "description": "The price of this book"
            }
        }
}
```

Listing 7-30. /schemas/booksale.js

```
module.exports = {
        "id": "BookSale",
        "properties": {
                "date": {
                        "type":"date",
                        "description": "Date of the transaction"
                },
                "books": {
                        "type": "array",
                        "description": "Books sold",
```

```
                    "items": {
                            "$ref": "Book"
                    }
            },
            "store": {
                    "type": "object",
                    "description": "The store where this sale took
                                    place",
                    "type": "object",
                    "$ref": "Store"
            },
            "employee": {
                    "type": "object",
                    "description": "The employee who makes the sale",
                    "$ref": "Employee"
            },
            "client": {
                    "type": "object",
                    "description": "The person who gets the books",
                    "$ref": "Client",
            },
            "totalAmount": {
                    "type": "integer"
            }

        }
}
```

Listing 7-31. /schemas/client.js

```
module.exports = {
        "id": "Client",
        "properties": {
                "name": {
                        "type": "string",
                        "description": "Full name of the client"
                },
```

```
                "address": {
                        "type": "string",
                        "description": "Address of residence of this
                                        client"
                },
                "phone_number": {
                        "type": "string",
                        "description": "Contact phone number for the
                                        client"
                },
                "email": {
                        "type": "string",
                        "description": "Email of the client"
                }
        }
}
```

Listing 7-32. /schemas/employee.js

```
module.exports = {
        "id": "Employee",
        "properties": {
                "first_name": {
                        "type": "string",
                        "description": "First name of the employee"
                },
                "last_name": {
                        "type": "string",
                        "description": "Last name of the employee"
                },
                "birthdate": {
                        "type": "string",
                        "description": "Date of birth of this employee"
                },
                "address": {
                        "type": "string",
```

```
                "description": "Address for the employee"
        },
        "phone_numbers": {
                "type": "array",
                "description": "List of phone numbers of this
                                    employee",
                "items": {
                        "type": "string"
                }
        },
        "email": {
                "type": "string",
                "description": "Employee's email"
        },
        "hire_date": {
                "type": "string",
                "description": "Date when this employee was hired"
        },
        "employee_number": {
                "type": "number",
                "description": "Unique identifier of the employee"
        }
    }
}
```

Listing 7-33. /schemas/store.js

```
module.exports = {
        "id": "Store",
        "properties": {
                "name": {
                        "type": "string",
                        "description": "The actual name of the store"
                },
                "address": {
                        "type": "string",
```

```
                        "description": "The address of the store"
            },
            "state": {
                    "type": "string",
                    "description": "The state where the store resides"
            },
            "phone_numbers": {
                    "type": "array",
                    "description": "List of phone numbers for the
                                    store",
                    "items": {
                            "type": "string"
                    }
            },
            "employees": {
                    "type": "array",
                    "description": "List of employees of the store",
                    "items": {
                            "$ref": "Employee"
                    }
            }
        }
    }
}
```

swagger-ui

This folder contains the downloaded Swagger UI project, so we will not go over this
particular code; however, I will mention the minor modifications we'll need to do to the
index.html file (located at the root of the swagger-ui folder) to get the UI to properly load.

The changes needed are three very simple ones:

1. Edit the routes for all the resources loaded (CSS and JS files) to
    start with /swagger-ui/. In other words, all loaded resources
    should look like the following:

    ```
    <link href='/swagger-ui/css/screen.css' media='print'
    rel='stylesheet' type='text/css'/>
    ```

2. Change the URL for the documentation server to `http://localhost:9000/api-docs` (around line 31).

3. Uncomment the block of code in line 73. Set the right value to the apiKey variable (set it to 777).

With those changes, the UI should be able to load correctly and allow you to start testing your API.

Root Folder

This is the root of the project. There are only two files here: the main `index.js` and the `package.json` file that contains the dependencies and other project attributes.

Listing 7-34. /package.json

```json
{
  "name": "come_n_read",
  "version": "1.0.0",
  "description": "",
  "main": "index.js",
  "scripts": {
    "test": "echo \"Error: no test specified\" && exit 1"
  },
  "author": "",
  "license": "ISC",
  "dependencies": {
    "colors": "^1.0.3",
    "config": "^1.30.0",
    "halson": "^2.3.1",
    "mongoose": "^5.0.0",
    "mongoose-json-select": "^0.2.1",
    "mongoose-mock": "^0.4.0",
    "proxyquire": "^2.0.1",
    "restify": "^6.0.0",
    "restify-errors": "^6.0.0",
    "restify-plugins": "^1.6.0",
```

```
    "sinon": "^4.5.0",
    "swagger-node-restify": "^0.1.2",
    "tv4": "^1.1.9",
    "tv4-formats": "^1.0.0",
    "underscore": "^1.7.0",
    "winston": "^3.0.0-rc2"

  }
}
```

The most interesting part of this file is the list of dependencies. The rest was autogenerated using the init option of the npm command-line tool.

Tip   If you're testing out the code for this chapter, make sure you install all dependencies listed in this file by running npm `install` from the root of the project's folder.

Listing 7-35. /index.js

```
const restify = require("restify"),
        restifyPlugins = restify.plugins,
        colors = require("colors"),
        lib = require("./lib"),
        swagger = require("swagger-node-restify"),
        config = require("config");

const server = restify.createServer(config.get('server'))

server.use(restifyPlugins.queryParser({
        mapParams: true
}))
server.use(restifyPlugins.bodyParser())

restify.defaultResponseHeaders = data => {
  this.header('Access-Control-Allow-Origin', '*')
}
```

```
///Middleware to check for valid api key sent
server.use((req, res, next) => {
        //We move forward if we're dealing with the swagger-ui
        or a valid key
        if(req.url.indexOf("swagger-ui") != -1 || lib.helpers.
validateKey(req.headers.hmacdata || '', req.params.api_key, lib)) {
                next()
        } else {
                res.send(401, { error: true, msg: 'Invalid api key sent'})
        }
})

/**
Validate each request, as long as there is a schema for it
*/
server.use((req, res, next) => {
        let results = lib.schemaValidator.validateRequest(req)
        if(results.valid) {
                return next()
        }
        res.send(400, results)
})

//the swagger-ui is inside the "swagger-ui" folder
server.get(/^\/swagger-ui(\/.*)?/, restifyPlugins.serveStatic({
        directory: __dirname + '/',
        default: 'index.html'
 }))

swagger.addModels(lib.schemas)
swagger.setAppHandler(server)
lib.helpers.setupRoutes(server, swagger, lib)

swagger.configureSwaggerPaths("", "/api-docs", "") //we remove the {format}
part of the paths, to
swagger.configure('http://localhost:9000', '0.1')
```

```
server.listen(config.get('server.port'), () => {
        lib.logger.info("Server started succesfully...")
        lib.db.connect( err => {
                if(err) lib.logger.error("Error trying to connect to
                database: ", err)
                else lib.logger.info("Database service successfully started")
        })
})
```

And finally, the main file, the one that starts it all up is the index.js. There are four distinct sections to this file:

1. The *initial section*, which requires all needed modules and instantiates the server.

2. The *middleware setup section*, which handles setting up all pieces of middleware (we'll go over this in a bit).

3. The *setup section*, which handles loading models, controllers, setting up routes, and whatnot.

4. The *server start section*, which starts the web server and the database client.

The initial and final sections of the file don't really require much explanation since they're pretty self-explanatory, so let's go over the other two.

Middleware Setup

The middleware setup is potentially the most important part of the file and of the bootstrap process required for the API to start up and function properly. But thanks to the ease of use and simplicity that the middleware mechanics bring to the table, it's very easy to write and understand.

We're setting up five different middleware here:

1. The *query parser* to turn the query parameters into an object so that we can access them easily

2. The *body parser* so that we can access the content of the POST and PUT requests as an object, with the added bonus of autoparsing JSON strings

3. The *security check*, which takes care of rehashing the request every time to make sure that we're dealing with an authenticated client

4. The *validate check*, which validates the request against any existing JSON Schema

5. The *static content folder*, which is not exactly a middleware, but acts as one for one specific set of routes, allowing Restify to serve static content

Setup Section

This last section is also very important; those five lines actually handle instantiating all the models, linking Swagger and the Restify server, setting up all the routes (linking the code of each action to the corresponding path and method defined in the spec section), and, finally, setting up the route for the Swagger back-end server.

Summary

Congratulations! You should now have a working version of our API, capable of doing pretty much everything we set up to do in Chapter 6. You should also have a better understanding of how these modules work. Ideally, you'll consider them for your next project. Of course, there are alternatives like the ones discussed in Chapter 5, so don't forget about those either.

In the final chapter of the book, I'll go over some of the most common issues you might encounter when dealing with this type of project, and you'll see how to solve them.

CHAPTER 8

Testing your API

It's time to take a small break from REST and API design to discuss something equally important for your project: how are you going to test it?

The entire point of this chapter is to give you a little insight into what we normally mean by "testing" in the context of software development. I'll cover some basic principles such as unit testing, mocking, and so forth, and once you're ready, we'll go over some examples of how to implement those concepts in your Node.js project.

So let's get started.

Testing 101

First things first: I'm going to be covering unit testing in this chapter, but if by the end of it you want to know more, please feel free to go online and keep reading. Honestly, there is more than enough material about this subject to fill several books. This chapter's only aim is to act as an entry way into this world.

The Definition

Let's start with the basics: at its core, testing in the context of software development is basically the act of formulating a statement (that should be true) about a piece of code and adding the required set of assertions to make sure we can prove that said statement is actually true. So a test can be something like Listing 8-1.

Listing 8-1. Pseudo-Code for a Theoretical Test Case

```
Statement: "myFunction" is capable of adding up two natural numbers
Assertions:
var a = 10;
var b = 2;
assertion(myFunction(a, b), "is equal to", a + b)
```

© Fernando Doglio 2018
F. Doglio, *REST API Development with Node.js*, https://doi.org/10.1007/978-1-4842-3715-1_8

We're not focusing on a specific language right now, so Listing 8-1 is only showing a pseudo-code attempt at what a test would look like. From that example, I should also note how I'm testing the function directly; it is a simple example and there is not a lot of context, but the point here is that your tests shuld focus on the smallest bit of code that makes sense, instead of testing several things at the same time. Let me explain with another example in Listing 8-2.

Listing 8-2. Several Different Assertions Inside the Same Test

```
Statement: "myFunction" can add, multiply and substract two natural numbers
Assertions:
var a = 10
var b = 10
assertion(myFunction("add", a, b), "is equal to", a + b)
assertion(myFunction("multiply", a, b), "is equal to", a * b)
assertion(myFunction("substract", a, b), "is equal to", a - b)
```

The example is still quite simple, but I've added a bit of a more complex internal logic to the function called myFunction by adding the ability to pass in the mathematical function to apply as the first parameter. With this new logic, the function we're testing is bigger, and it does do different things, so if we design our tests like in Listing 8-2, we can run into a problem: what happens if our test fails?

I haven't really covered what it means to "run" our tests, but it should be pretty obvious by now: your code gets executed and the assertions are verified, if they are true, then your test will succeed, but if they fail (i.e., your assertion stated two values were to be equal and, in practice, they aren't) then your entire test fails. You can see how that can be a problem if you're actually testing several things inside the same test. Once you get the results back from the execution, you'll have to dig deeper into the execution logs (if there are any) to actually understand where your problem lies.

To properly test a function like the new myFunction, you'd be better off by splitting your test case (which is how you call a single test) into three different ones, as seen in Listing 8-3:

Listing 8-3. Correct Way to Structure Test Cases When the Function Tested is Too Complex

```
Statement: "myFunction" can add two natural numbers
var a = 10
var b = 10
assertion(myFunction("add", a, b), "is equal to", a+b)

Statement: "myFunction" can multiply two natural numbers
var a = 10
var b = 10
assertion(myFunction("multiply", a, b), "is equal to", a*b)

Statement: "myFunction" can substract two natural numbers
var a = 10
var b = 10
assertion(myFunction("substract", a, b), "is equal to", a-b)
```

Now whenever your tests fails, you'll get better details from your test runner, because you'll know exactly which test failed, and thus, you'll be able to immediatly determine which block of code inside your complex function failed.

So to recap and to give you more of a *technical* definition of what unit testing is, from everything I've shown you so far, you could probably say that:

> *A unit test is a statement about a unit of code that needs to be proven true in order to pass.*

And the word *unit* is probably the most important one, because if you go online, you'll probably find a lot of people defining it (in this context of course) as your functions (provided you're using a procedural programming language) or your methods (if you're on an OOP language). But as you can see from a simple generic and pseudo-code-based example, a *unit* of code can actually be smaller than that. It's true that in all these examples I didn't really show the actual code of the function, and you could argue that for each test case of Listing 8-3, our function is actually calling other, smaller functions, and that is a very good point!

But, there is also probably code tying all those calls together (some kind of logic based on the value of your first parameter), so if you were to individually test those smaller functions instead, you'd be missing possible bugs. So if we go back to our definition of *unit,* you'd probably want something like the following (in the context of software testing ofcourse):

> *A unit of code is the smallest block of code that makes sense to test and would allow you to cover a whole logical path.*

So putting both definitions together, you get a pretty acurate idea of what testing your code means and a good basis for the rest of this chapter.

The Tools

Now that we've covered what it is, let's review the tools provided by this methodology that will allow you to test your code.

These are not software tools, these aren't libraries or frameworks you can use, we're not there yet. What I'm trying to give you here are the wheels you'll use to build your car down the road.

Test Cases & Test Suites

Test cases have already been covered, but to reiterate, it is how you call the actual test. You normally structure them to test a very specific scenario, which is why normally you'd need several cases before being sure you've properly covered every logical path inside your code.

Test suites are, as their name implies, groups of test cases. Depending on your system and your methodology, you might want to have a single test suite for all your tests or a set of suites, acting as logical groups for your unit tests. The criteria used for the suites is all up to you and your team, so feel free to use this tool to organize your code as much as you can.

Assertions

I've already used this concept in the previous section without formally defining because it's one of those things you don't really need to define before people can understand it. That being said, there are still some details I left out, so let me cover them here.

Assertions bring meaning to your test cases, everything else inside your test is just preparation for this line(s) of code. In other words, you first set everything up (function imports, variables, correct values, etc), and then state your assumptions about the outcome of the tested code, and that is your assertion.

If you want to get a bit more technical, an assertion is (usually) a function or method that executes your target code with the right parameters and checks its output against your expectations. If they match, then it makes your test pass; if they don't, then it spits out an error using the information it knows about your test (description, function called, expected value, and actual value are some of the most common ones).

You don't usually need to worry about creating assertions. They are part of every testing framework and library out there, all you need to know is how to use them, and that will depend on each implementation. Usually testing frameworks provide several flavors of assertions to help make the test cases' code more readable. So you might find yourself using assertions called `isTrue`, `isEqual`, `notEqual`, `throwsException` and other similar names, instead of using just one like in my previous examples. They are of course syntactic sugar, but when it comes to test development, making them readable and easy to understand is considered a very good practice.

And since we're in the topic of good practice for assertions, it is also considered a very good one to structure your test cases in a way that you only have one assertion per test. This will help you to:

- Keep your test's code clean and simple.

- Help the code to be readable.

- Simplify debugging when one of the tests fails, since there is only one thing that can fail per test.

Stubs, Mocks, Spies, and Dummies

These are all similar tools, so I wanted to cover them as part of the same section since they're all related in one way or another. It's important to note that so far the examples provided in this chapter have been quite simple and naive. Usually production systems aren't that straighforward, your methods and functions will normally interact with each other and other external services (such as APIs, Databases, even the filesystem). This is why this set of particular tools will help you out in that aspect.

One key mantra that you need to repeat over and over when writing tests is:

I shall not test code that's already been tested by others

And even though in theory it's quite obvious (I mean, why would you? Really?), in practice, the line is sometimes a little blurry. One very common case, especially when writing public APIs, is to use databases; your CRUD methods, for instance, will most likely be 80% database interaction, so should you test that code? The answer is "not entirely." Let me give you an example with Listing 8-4:

Listing 8-4. Generic "Save" Function Interacting with Your Database

```
function savePerson(person) {
        if(validationFunction(person)) {
                query = createSavePersonQuery(person)
                return executeQuery(query)
        } else {
                return false
        }
}
```

Listing 8-4 shows a very basic database interaction, you have several functions there that you probably already tested individually because of their complexity (validationFunction and createSavePersonQuery) and you also have a function called executeQuery, which in our case is provided by your database library. You didn't write that function, you don't even have access to its code, so why would you care about testing it? You can't really do anything about it if it fails.

More so, why would you even consider depending on your database server being up and running? Are you going to be using the production database for your tests? What will you do with the garbage data generated by your tests? What if your database server is up, but your table is not created? Will the test fail? Should it?

These are all normal questions that arise when starting to write tests and hitting the brick wall that is reality. If you're not just starting with tests, but with software development in general you might think that the right way to go is to have a "test database," one you can control and you can do whatever you want with. Heck! I've done it, it's completely normal, but also **wrong**.

You see, when you add an external service into your tests, even one you think you can control such as your own database server, you're implicitly testing that service and the connectivity between both systems inside your unit test. You've turned a simple and straightforward test into a very complex one that is not even prepared to handle everything that could go wrong. What if your network fails? Should this test fail? What if you forgot to start your db server? Should this test fail too? See where I'm going with this? And I'm just giving you one simple example, one database. I'm not covering logging, other APIs, multiple database queries, and so forth. You *definitely* need to cut all connections to the *outside* when unit testing, and that means everything that is not your target unit of code (or put another way, each test that you write should take care of only one unit of code and nothing else). Fear not though, because here is where this particular set of tools comes into play.

Stubs

Let's say your target unit of code for a particular test depends on another function call, so whatever that function returns, your code will react accordingly. And you need to add tests for all the possible reactions, how can you ensure the function you depend on actually returns what you want?

One possible solution would be to simply use the "right" values, if you already know how this function behaves, you can do that, but if someone else changes the function in the future, your tests will fail, because they depend on the actual implementation of an external function.

Enter stubs, these guys help you deal with external services (or more like external function calls) by replacing the code that uses them with a simpler version that instead, returns a known and controlled value. Or, put another way, you can re-write the functions you depend on to make sure they return the value you expect them to.

You can stub a function or a method in a particular object (as long as the language lets you), so instead of controlling the database and its content (like in the previous example), you would overwrite the function that does the actual query with one that controls the output to whatever you need it to be (as seen in Listing 8-5). This way you can safely test all possible cases (including those when the network connectivity fails, or the database is down).

Listing 8-5. Pseudo-Code Examples of How Stubs Help Your Tests

```
Statement: when the person is saved, the function should return TRUE
Stub: executeQuery(q) { return TRUE } //we assume the query execution went
well
var person = {name: "Fernando Doglio", age: 34}
assertion(savePerson(person), "equals to", TRUE)

Statement: when the person's data is not valid, the function should return
FALSE
Stub: validationFunction(data) {return FALSE} //we need the validation to
fail in this case
var person = {name: "Fernando Doglio", age: 34}
assertion(savePerson(person), "equals to", FALSE)
```

Listing 8-5 shows two examples of why stubs are so useful. The first one shows how you can easily control the outcome of the interaction with an external service; you don't need complex logic inside your stubs, the important part on them is their returned value. The second example is not overwriting an external service, but, rather, an external function—in fact, one that you probably wrote. And the reason for that (instead of simply providing an invalid person object as input) is that in the future, your validation code could change; maybe you added or removed valid parameters from your person definition, and now your test could fail, not due to the code you're testing but to an unwanted side effect. So instead of suffering from that, you simply eliminate the dependency on that function and make sure that no matter what happens to the internal logic of validationFunction, you'll always handle the FALSE output correctly.

In fact, both examples from Listing 8-5 show the two most common uses for stubs:

1. Removing dependency from external service

2. Forcing a logical path inside your target test code

Mocks

Mocks are very similar to stubs, so much so in fact, that many people use both terms to refer to the same behavior. But that is not correct, even though they're both conceptually similar, they are also different.

While stubs allow you to replace or redefine a function or a method (or even an entire object, why not?), mocks allow you to set expected behaviors on real objects/functions. So you're not technically replacing the object or function, you're just telling it what to do in some very specific cases. Other than that, the object remains working as usual.

Let's look at Listing 8-6 to understand the definition.

Listing 8-6. Example of How a Mock Could Be Used Inside a Test Case

```
Statement: When replenishing the diapers aisle, the same amount added needs
to be removed from the inventory
Code:
var inventory = Mock(Inventory("diapers"))
//set expectations
inventory
```

```
    .expect("getItems", 100)
    .returns(TRUE)
    .expect("removeFromInventory", 100)
    .returns(TRUE)

var aisle = Aisle("diapers")
aisle.setRequiredItems(100)
aisle.replenish(inventory) //executes the normal flow
assertion(aisle.isFull(),"equals to", TRUE)
assertion(inventory.verifiedBehavior, "equals to", TRUE)
```

I know, I know, two assertions inside the same test case. I haven't even finished the chapter and I'm already going against my words. Bear with me here, in some cases the expected behavior for mocks is automatically checked by whatever framework you're using, so this example is just to let you know it's happening. Now get off my back!

Now, back to the example on Listing 8-6, we could've definitely done this with stubs too, but we're *conceptually* testing something different. Not just the final state of the aisle object, but also the way that the aisle object interacts with the inventory, which is a bit harder to do with stubs. During the first part of the test, where we set the expectations, we're basically telling the mocked object, that its getItems method should be called with a 100 as a parameter and that when it happens, it should return TRUE. We're also telling it that its removeFromInventory method should be called with a 100 as parameter and to return TRUE when this happens. In the end, we're just checking to see if that actually happened.

Spies

As cool as this name might sound to you, we're still dealing with special objects for your test cases. This particular type of object is an evolution of the stubs. And the reason why I'm just mentioning it is because spies are the answer to the example on the mock section.

In other words, spies are stubs that gather execution information, so they can tell you, at the end, what got called, when, and with which parameters. There is not much to them, we can look at another example (see Listing 8-7) where you'd need to know information about the execution of a function in order to show you how you could test it with spies.

Listing 8-7. Example of a Spy Being Used to Determine if a Method was Called

```
Statement: FileReader should close the open file after it's done.
Code:
var filename = "yourfile.txt"
var myspy = new Spy(IOModule, "openFile") //create a spy for the method
openFile in the module dedicated to I/O
var reader = new FileReader(filename, IOModule)
reader.read()

assertion(myspy.calledWith(filename), "equals to", TRUE)
```

The example in Listing 8-7 should probably be one of many tests for the FileReader module, but it exemplifies when a spy can come in handy. In this particular example, we're making sure the right method is called to open a file, and that we're passing it the right value (the content of the `filename` variable).

Note   The spy, unlike the stub, wraps the target method/function, instead of replacing it, so the original code of your target will also be executed.

Dummies

Dummies are simply objects that serve no real purpose other than being there when they're required. They are never really used, but in some cases, such as strongly typed languages, you might need to create dummy objects for your method calls to be possible.

If you're creating a stub of a method that receives three parameters, even though you're not thinking about using them, you might need to create dummies so they can be eventually passed to it. This is a very simple case of test utility object, but it's a name that also gets mentioned quite a bit, so I thought I'd cover it.

Fixtures

Test fixtures help provide the initial state of your system before your tests get executed. They come in handy when your tested code depends on several outside sources of data.

For instance, think of a configuration checker for your system, you could have fixtures for different versions of your config files, and load one in each test case, depending on the type of output you'd want to test.

Fixtures are usually loaded before the tests are run and can be unloaded (or reverted if necessary) after everything has been tested. Usually test frameworks provide specific instances on the testing flow for these cases, so you just need to add your fixture-related code in there.

Best Practices

I've already covered some of these partially in the previous section of this chapter, but it's probably a good idea to review the full list of recommendations when writing tests. You have to remember that like anything in software development, it's never a solo effort, even if you're the only one writing code right now, you have to think about the future.

So let's quickly review and recap.

- **Consistent**: Your test cases need to be consistent, in the sense that no matter how many times you run them, they always need to return the same result if the tested code hasn't changed.

- **Atomic**: The end result of your tests need to be either a PASS or a FAIL message; that's it, there is no middleground here.

- **Single responsibility**: This one we already discussed. Your tests should be taking care of one logical path, just one, that way their output is easy to understand.

- **Useful assertion messages**: Testing frameworks usually provide a way for you to enter descriptions of your test suites and test cases, that way they can be used when a test fails.

- **No conditional logic inside it**: Again, I mentioned this one in an earlier section; you don't want to add complex logic inside the test case, it is only meant to initialize and verify end results. If you see yourself adding this type of code into your test cases, then it's probably time to split this one into two (or more) new ones.

- **No exception handling** (unless that is what you're looking for): This one is related to the previous one; if you're writing tests, you shouldn't really care about any exceptions thrown by our code, there should already be code in place to catch them. Unless, of course, you're actually testing that your code throws a specific exception, in which case, disregard this one.

Testing with Node.js

Now that you've got an idea of what unit testing is and the basic concepts behind this practice, we can move forward with a specific implementation. You'll see that testing your code in Node is not hard at all, even without libraries, since the language already comes with a built-in assertion module ready to be used.

Testing Without Modules

Let me first talk about this option, it's probably not the way to go, since the provided module is pretty basic, but if you're looking for something that's quick and dirty, this will do the job.

One of the major things you'll notice in this library is that it's missing the rest of the framework. By requiring it in your code, you only get the assertion support, the rest of the helper functions will have to come from you or someplace else. That being said, let's look into it anyway.

As I already mentioned, this module does not require any kind of installation steps, since it's already provided with Node's installation, and all you have to do to use it is to require the module `assert`. After you do so, you'll gain access to a set of assertion methods, which basically help you compare two values (or objects).

I'm going to list some of the most interesting ones. If you want the see the full list, please go to the official documentation.[1]

---

[1]https://nodejs.org/api/assert.html

ok(value[, message])

This method evaluates value and if it's truthy, it'll pass, otherwise it'll throw an AssertionError. The message (if set) is set as the message of the exception. This one performs a simple equality validation (using ==), so if you need to check strict equality, then you might want to go with the strictEqual method.

When dealing with truthy values, you have to remember what that means for your specific language. In the case of JavaScript, this is what you'd get when calling ok:

- ok(1) = TRUE

- ok(0) = FALSE

- ok("hello world!") = TRUE

- ok("") = FALSE

- ok(undefined) = FALSE

- ok(3203) = TRUE

- ok(null) = FALSE

deepStrictEqual(actual, expected[, message])

This one performs a deep comparison between two objects. In case you didn't know, that means is Node will recursively compare (using the strictly equal operand) properties inside the objects, and if that comparison fails it'll throw an AssertionError.

For instance, something like what's shown on Listing 8-8 would show an error message.

Listing 8-8. Simple Example of how deepStrictEqual Works

```
const assert = require("assert")
try {
        assert.deepStrictEqual({a: 1}, {a: '1'})
} catch(e) {
        console.log(e)
}
```

The previous example shows the details of the thrown exception:

Listing 8-9. AssertionError Exception Thrown from the Code of Listing 8-8

```
{ AssertionError [ERR_ASSERTION]: { a: 1 } deepStrictEqual { a: '1' }
    at repl:1:14
    at ContextifyScript.Script.runInThisContext (vm.js:44:33)
    at REPLServer.defaultEval (repl.js:239:29)
    at bound (domain.js:301:14)
    at REPLServer.runBound [as eval] (domain.js:314:12)
    at REPLServer.onLine (repl.js:433:10)
    at emitOne (events.js:120:20)
    at REPLServer.emit (events.js:210:7)
    at REPLServer.Interface._onLine (readline.js:278:10)
    at REPLServer.Interface._line (readline.js:625:8)
  generatedMessage: true,
  name: 'AssertionError [ERR_ASSERTION]',
  code: 'ERR_ASSERTION',
  actual: { a: 1 },
  expected: { a: '1' },
  operator: 'deepStrictEqual' }
```

As expected, because in Javascript the number 1 and the string literal '1' aren't strictly the same, the objects compared in Listing 8-8 aren't equal.

Note   If instead you were to use the deepEqual method, the comparison from Listing 8-8 would pass correctly.

---

throws(block[, error][, message)

The other method I want to highlight is this one, which will test your block of code for a thrown exception. The only mandatory parameter here is (like the method signature indicates) the first one, but you can also add pretty interesting behaviors using the second one.

For the error parameter, you can use one of several options, such as a constructor that simply indicates the type of error expected. You can also use a RegEx to validate the name of the type or, and this is the most crazy you can get with this method, you can manually check the results by providing a checking function as the second parameter. Listing 8-10 shows a small example taken directly from Node's documentation site, showing how to use a function to check a couple of details about the error thrown.

Listing 8-10. Code Showing Example Using a Function As a Second Parameter

```
assert.throws(
  () => {
    throw new Error('Wrong value');
  },
  function(err) {
    if ((err instanceof Error) && /value/.test(err)) {
      return true;
    }
  },
  'unexpected error'
);
```

There are a lot of other methods to use but they're just variations on the three we just covered, so I'll let you browse the documentation to read the whole list of options. Let's now look at what it looks like to add tests in Node using one of the most common libraries out there: Mocha.

Mocha

When it comes to testing libraries for Node, the list is always growing: you have some that add assertions, others that are full testing frameworks for TDD, others provide the tools you need if you're practicing BDD, and I could keep going. So, let's just focus on one of them, the one most people in the community seem to be using these days, and see what testing with it looks like.

So particularily, Mocha[2] is a testing framework (so it's not just an assertion library, it actually provides a full set of tools for us) that allows for both asynchronous and

---

[2]https://mochajs.org/

synchrounous testing; so considering asynchronous functions are quite common in Node.js, this is a great choice already.

Installing and First Steps

To install the latest version of Mocha into your system, you can simply use the command shown in Listing 8-11:

Listing 8-11. Installing Mocha

```
$ npm install mocha -g
```

Listing 8-11 will install version 5.1.0 as of the writing of this chapter. Once this is over, you can proceed to start writing your test cases. Listing 8-12 shows a quick example of one:

Listing 8-12. Sample Test Case Written Using Mocha

```
const assert = require('assert');
describe('Array', function() {
  describe('#indexOf()', function() {
    it('should return -1 when the value is not present', function() {
      assert.equal([1,2,3].indexOf(4), -1);
    });
  });
});
```

There are several things to notice from the example on Listing 8-12:

- We're not directly calling mocha, or requiring the module at all. This is not needed, because to execute the test, you'll be using mocha's cli tool, which will take care of that.

- We're back to using the `assert` module from Node, which is one of the features from Mocha: it won't force an assertion syntax on you, it'll let you decide which one to use based on your prefererences.

- The `describe` function can be nested as many times as you need, it's just a gruping mechanism that can help you when reading the code and when looking at the output from mocha (more on this subject in a minute).

- Finally, the it function, on the other hand, contains the actual test case; inside its callback you define the test's logic.

To run the test, then you simply execute:

```
$ mocha
```

and the output should be something like the one shown in Listing 8-13 (provided you saved your code in a file called test.js, which is where mocha will look by default for your tests):

Listing 8-13. Output from Running Your Mocha Tests

```
Array
  #indexOf()
    ✓ should return -1 when the value is not present
1 passing (7ms)
```

Notice the indentation of the first two lines; that's related to the use of the describe function.

Testing Asynchronous Code

Before going into the specifics of how to test our project, I'm going to talk about one more feature provided by Mocha, since it'll come in super handy: asynchronous tests.

To test asynchronous functions using Mocha, you simply have to add a parameter to the callback on the it function. This will tell Mocha that the test is asynchronous, and it'll know to wait until that parameter is called upon (it's going to be a function indicating the end of the test). It is worth noting that this function can only be called once per test, so if you try (or do so by accident) to call it more than once, your test will fail.

Listing 8-14 provides an example of how this would look.

Listing 8-14. Example of an Asynchronous Test Case in Mocha

```
describe('User', function() {
  describe('#save()', function() {
    it('should save without error', function(done) {
      var user = new User('Luna');
      user.save(function(err) {
        if (err) done(err);
        else done();
```

```
      });
    });
  });
});
```

The attribute for the callback is usually called done, to signify the ending of the particular test case. Finally, this function follows the normal callback pattern, so it receives the error attribute as the first parameter, thus the code from Listing 8-15 can be further simplified as follows:

Listing 8-15. Simplified Example of an Asynchronous Test Case

```
describe('User', function() {
  describe('#save()', function() {
    it('should save without error', function(done) {
      var user = new User('Luna');
      user.save(done);
    });
  });
});
```

There are a ton of other features for this library that I haven't covered (and won't cover) in this chapter, so please, I urge you to go to its main website[3] and browse through its documentation. Let's now look at what it would look like to add some tests to our API project.

Testing Our API

In this section we're going to cover how to go about adding all the required code into the existing API project, so that we can test it's code.

Because of the nature of the API project, there is a lot of repeated code/logic, such as the create methods, in each one. The same code an eventually be isolated and individually tested before it gets out of hand.

For the purpose of this exercise and to show you how you can add tests yourself (applying the concepts we've already covered), I'm going to show you how to create tests for the create method of the BookSales controller.

---

[3]See https://mochajs.org/#table-of-contents

Let's look at the code first (in Listing 8-16), and then I'll do a quick overview of what's being presented.

Listing 8-16. Unit Tests for the BookSales Controller's Create Method

```
const assert = require("assert");
const restifyErrors = require("restify-errors")
const sinon = require("sinon")
const mongoose = require("mongoose")
const lib = require("../lib");

describe("Controllers", function () {
        describe("BookSales", function() {
                describe("#create", function() {

                    let BookSales;

                    //setup all we need for the tests
                    beforeEach(function() {
                            BookSales = require("../controllers/
                            booksales")(lib);
                            sinon.spy(BookSales, "writeHAL")
                    })

                    //and tear down whatever we changed
                    afterEach(function(){
                            BookSales.writeHAL.restore();
                    })

                    //tests
                    it("should return an InvalidArgument exception
                    if no body is provided in the request", function
                    (done) {
                            BookSales.create({}, {}, function(err) {
                                    assert.ok(err instanceof
                                    restifyErrors.InvalidArgumentError)
                                    done();
                            })
                    })
                })
```

```
                    it("should call the save method for the booksale
                    model", function() {
                            //we'll spy on this method to understand
                            when and how we call it
                            sinon.spy(mongoose.Model.prototype, "save")

                            BookSales.create({body: {totalAmount: 1}}, {})
                            assert.ok(mongoose.Model.prototype.save.
                            calledOnce)

                            mongoose.Model.prototype.save.restore();
                    })

                    it("should call the writeHAL method", function() {
                            //we stub the method, so it can actually
                            succeed even without a valid connection
                            sinon.stub(mongoose.Model.prototype,
                            "save").callsFake( cb => cb() )
                            //we create a simple fake "json" property
                            that will be called by writeHAL
                            BookSales.create({body: {totalAmount: 1}},
                            {json: () => {} })
                            assert.ok(BookSales.writeHAL.calledOnce)
                            mongoose.Model.prototype.save.restore();
                    })
            })
        })
})
```

So we begin by creating the groups for our tests. As I mentioned before, these groups can be anything we want. In my case I felt Controllers -> [Controller name] -> [Method name] would come in handy.

After that, for the specific method we're testing here, we'll test the following:

- That it throws the correct type of error message whenever the body for a new book sale is not present

- That it calls the save method on the model being created

- Finally, that after a successful data save on the database, the controller is actually calling the writeHAL method, to create the correctly formatted response

All three tests have different mechanics. The first shows you how to use the *done* callback optionally available within each test. If you're dealing with an asynchronous function, that's how you tell it when to actually stop waiting for a response.

The second is actually creating a spy on a method, so we can tell whether or not it was called. Note that to create the spy, we're using yet another module called SinonJS (which you can install by simply doing npm install sinon). This particular library works together with Mocha (or any other unit testing framework) and provides the of the mejor tools we saw earlier in this chapter: Mocks, Spies, and Stubs.

Finally, the third test case is creating a *stub*, because we need to control exactly how the insertion into the database works (in this case, ending with a successful returned value as if the database was actually there). This particular test is also not directly creating and restoring the spy on the writeHAL method for the controller; instead, that happens inside the beforeEach and afterEach function callbacks, which are part of the testing flow executed by Mocha. They're there to move away from the test case's code anything that needs to happen for every single test.

Now that we've covered the code, let's quickly look at its output to understand what you should be aiming to get on your side. First, you execute it with the following line, assuming you've added the code from Listing 8-16 in a folder called "tests" at the root of your project.

```
$mocha tests/
```

And the output should be something like the following:

```
fernandodoglio@UY-IT00066 ~/workspace/personal/writing/rest-api-development (master) $ mocha tests/


   Controllers
      BookSales
         #create                                    log message for the first test
2018-04-19T04:03:54.368Z [Default] error: Error of type InvalidArgumentError found: Missing json data
            ✓ should return an InvalidArgument exception if no body is provided in the request
            ✓ should call the save method for the booksale model
            ✓ should call the writeHAL method


   3 passing (21ms)
```

Figure 8-1. *Output of the execution*

In Figure 8-1 you can see the other point of having the groups: the results are much easier to understand if the tests are properly grouped. Also, notice the error message; even though the tests are all green, we're showing an error message, and that's completely normal, since the very first test is actually testing for the error type.

Summary

This chapter covered a small glimpse into the unit testing world, showing you the basics to both understand how they work and how to write them, and how to implement them in Node.js.

In the next chapter, I'm going to cover the actual deployment of your application and the type of tools you might want to consider using for that.

Deploying into Production

As the last step in your normal development cycle, you'd want to deploy your brand new APIs into a production system. This might sound obvious to you (then again, maybe not), but just because it works on your computer doesn't mean it'll work for your customers, so when deploying into such a specific environment like Production, there are some key aspects you'd want to consider, and we'll review those in this chapter.

Finally and to close this chapter, we'll go over Shipit and PM2—a very interesting pair of tools to help you keep track of your production deploys.

Different Environments

When working on seriuos software project, basically anything that is intended to see the light of the public will normally have different stages. In particular, projects that are web-related, like, say, an API, will have these stages represented as different environments where the application is deployed.

In these environments, you'll have different versions of your code deployed and working, depending on the intended use of each one. Any standard web-related project will have at least three or maybe four environments to deploy to at any point into their development cycle.

The Classical Development Workflow

Based off of the content of Table 9-1, the classical development cycle for a web-related project looks something like Figure 9-1.

© Fernando Doglio 2018

F. Doglio, *REST API Development with Node.js*, https://doi.org/10.1007/978-1-4842-3715-1_9

Table 9-1. *List of Standard Environments for Web-Based Software Projects*

Environment	Description
Development	This environment is usually intended for developers only; here is where they normally integrate their currently in-progress work and see how it behaves with the rest of their colleagues' work. If there is only one developer working on the project, this could very well be his/her computer (provided the project being worked on is capable of running on a single computer).
QA (or sometimes, QC)	After the developer's work is done and they have deemed it *ready*, the code needs to be deployed here. In this environment the quality assurance team (or whoever is in charge of quality on your team) will review the feature from a functional point of view (or in other words, without looking at the source code).
UAT (sometimes this one is missing)	Also known as User Acceptance Tests, this environment is meant to act as a pre-production stage, where you'll have the code that is meant to go to production soon deployed. At this point your client or a subset of final customers will be testing this version of the product. The intention is to catch any issues that might've escaped your developers and your QA/QC team because is more of a business-related problem than a technical one.
Production	Last but certainly not least, production is where your ready-to-be-used code will live. This is the final stage of your development cycle.

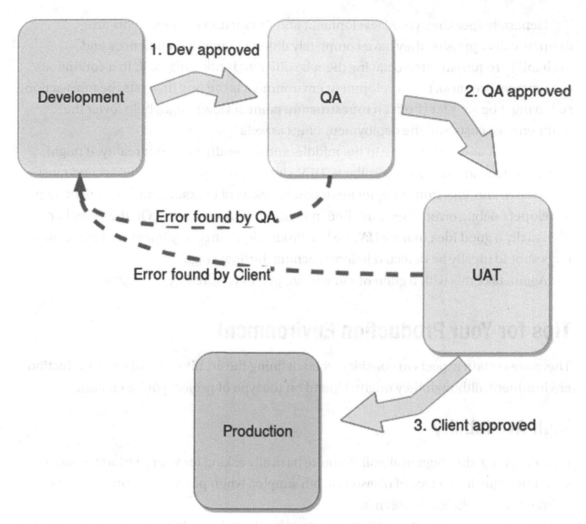

Figure 9-1. *Diagram describing a typical development cycle*

If everything goes well (which usually never happens, let's be real here), your code will go from the Development environment all the way to Production, one environment at the time. But if there are problems with the delivered code, they should be found either in the QA environment or in the UAT, although the latter is far from desired, since that potentially means exposing issues to the final client.

As for how similar or different these environments should be from each other, there is no real standard here, since that will definitely depend on the type of project you're working on, the budget you have, where these environments are located, and a big list of "etc." after this. I will, however, give you a basic rule of thumb.

Generally speaking, your Development and Production environments are diametrically opposite; they have completely different intended audiences and availability requirements, so having them be different is not a big deal. In a continuous deployment scenario, the development environment is the one that gets the most action, so having it be simpler (from an infrastructure point of view) might help lower the maintenance costs and the deployment times as well.

As for QA and UAT, they're in the middle, and depending on your reality, it might be a good idea to have QA be similar to DEV, since (a) it is going to be the second most active environment (from a deployment point of view, of course), and (b) it might help developers debug errors they can't find in their own environments. On the other hand, it's usually a good idea to have UAT be like Production, since any infrastructure-related bugs should ideally be detected before reaching the final stage.

Again, take this with a grain of salt and adapt it to your reality.

Tips for Your Production Environment

There are certain aspects to consider when defining the architecture of your production environment, although they might depend on the type of project you're creating.

High Availability

If you're going after high availablity, you're basically asking for your platform/system to stay functional in the face of disaster or, put simpler, when parts of your modules start failing due to technical problems.

Don't get me wrong, this subject alone is quite big and could fill up several chapters; I'm just doing a very high-level introduction and describing a couple of techniques that might come in handy when you start thinking about going live, and those are: load-balancing your web servers and thinking about zone availability. Let me go into a bit more details on them.

Load Balancers

On any normal and successful application that starts being massively used, your incoming traffic will become a problem if you're not prepared for it.

This traffic will start overloading your servers first, and when this happens, you'll either have to scale up vertically or horizontally. Vertical scale implies adding more resources to your servers (memory or disc, for instance) but that (obviously) has its limits. Eventually this strategy will not be enough.

Horizontal scaling, however, implies adding more computing power by adding more computers (or, in this case, servers). This is the better option if you know your traffic can keep growing to exceed the capacity of just one server, but is also adds extra problems.

When you have several web servers for your client-facing application, how do you distribute the load among them? This is where load balancer comes in.

Load balancers are software products you can install on your server, and they will (if properly configured) distribute incoming traffic into your array of servers. Some common load balancers are ELB from Amazon, F5 Networks, and Nginx (yes, the web server can also be configured as a load balancer). These load balancers work by distributing incoming traffic based on a pre-defined set of rules, such as:

- Round robin: With every new request the balancer would hit a new server, and it'll keep going by cycling to the first one.

- Least connected: Next incoming request will go to the server with the least number of active connections

- IP hash function: Hashing function of the client's IP address, assigning one hash code to each server

One caveat with using load balancers for web applications is that if your servers are stateful, you might run into a problem if you forgot about sticky sessions. But of course, you're building a RESTful API, which by definition is stateless, so this shouldn't be a problem, should it?

Just in case, let's review.

When dealing with user sessions, the web server creates an in-memory object that resides on the actual server that is serving your requests. This is all fine and dandy until you get multiple servers working in parallel and, in theory, interchangeably with one another. The problem here is that when you have all those servers with an in-memory version of your session, you can't really synchronize that data between all of them, so in the end as shown in Figure 9-2, they will have a partial version of the overall session information and, for most part, will render it useless to you.

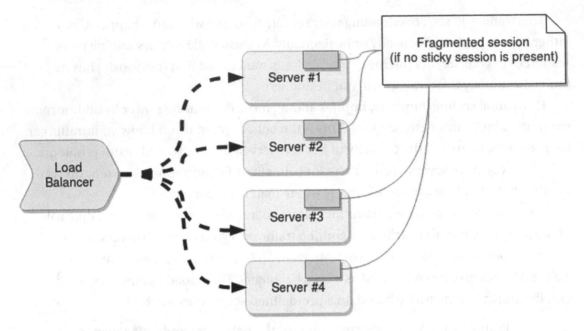

Figure 9-2. *Diagram showing classic problem with a fragmented session*

Enter sticky sessions: a way of letting your balancers know to keep one client associated to the same server after the first connection, that way the server-side session can be retrieved and updated on every request. This is a very well-known technique, and every load balancer has a way of dealing with this particular challenge.

You could also solve this by extracting your session management into a separate, common service, such as a database (see Figure 9-3), so every server would be able to access and update session data independently.

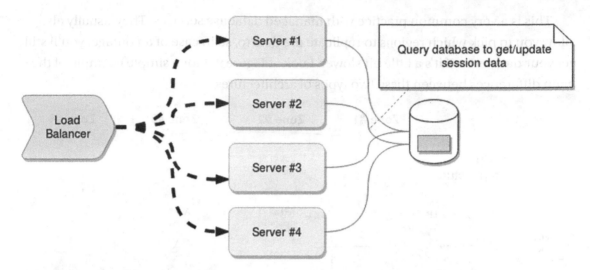

Figure 9-3. *Session information extracted into a common database*

The only caveat with this approach is the extra work required to get the servers working with the database (specially compared to using out-of-the-box features when dealing with in-memory sessions).

Zone Availablity

Another way of achieving high availability in your application, especially if you're deploying into a Cloud service, is the ability to have your deployment either spread or duplicated across multiple regions.

A very unpredictable and hard-to-overcome problem when you're dealing with hosting your applications with a third-party provider is that you don't have any control over their infrastructure, and if it fails, for any reason, you're affected, whether you like it or not.

None of the major cloud providers will agree to a 100% uptime SLA (Service Level Agreement, or put simply, and agreement between provider and consumer regarding quality of the service), so no matter who you're paying your hosting bills to, they will eventually fail to provide. And that is when multi-zone deployments come in handy, because usually downtimes on the cloud affect an entire geographical zone, so the only way to get around this problem is by having your deployments replicated or spread across several zones, effectively reducing the chances one of these geographical problems will affect you.

This is a very common practice with managed database services. They usually also allow you to pick which regions to replicate the data to, so in case of an outage, you'll still get your data, even if it's a little bit slower. Look at Figure 9-4 for a simple example of the main differences between these two types of architectures.

Figure 9-4. *Simple diagram showing the main differences between a replicated and a spread architecture*

Both options take advantage of multi-zone setups, and they effectively got you covered if something were to happen to some of the used zones. That being said, there are some core differences, and deciding which one is the best match for your project is completely up to you.

Let's quickly look at some pros and cons of each case in Table 9-2.

Table 9-2. *Pros and Cons of Both Deployment Models*

Deployment model	Pros	Cons
Replicated	• Easier deployment, everything deploys as one single block • You only need one LB to pick the right zone based on availability (at least, you could also have other criteria, such as latency). • Simpler client–platform communication	• Less flexibility when it comes to deployments and balancing strategies • If you're dealing with in-memory sessions, you need to configure sticky sessions or use the common database.
Spread	• Extra flexibility when it comes to zone-dependent deployments • Stronger fault tolerance. If API #1 fails, you don't lose the current transaction on API #2.	• A more complex deployment plan than the replicated model • Complex client–platform communication, since you'd most likely end up needing a load balancer configured for each pair of APIs.

Doing the Actual Deployment

After going over the basics, we're now ready to look at some of the tools available to us if we're the ones in charge of deploying our code into production (or any other environment, for that matter).

In this section I'll go over two tools that will help you while uploading your code into the server and then, once it's already up and deployed, help you manage your processes in production.

Shipit

Uploading your code to the server, whether it's on the cloud or something on-premise, can be as easy as an scp (a secure copy command that uses SSH authentication) or as complicated as following a 20-step playbook. Hoping for the first with microservice-based platforms is the the very definition of wishful thinking.

Fear not though, because there are many tools out there to help you automate complicated deployments; they might not be easy the first time around, but subsequent deployments should be considerably painless.

Shipit is exactly one of those tools, only one that is completely based on Node, so you don't need to install extra support for other languages in your system, something you would have to do if you were to use other common tools, such as Capistrano[1] (which requires Ruby to run).

With these tools, you can create simple tasks written in JavaScript that can then be orchestrated from the command line. To be more specific, Shipit is actually a combination of two tools: shipit-cli and shipit-deploy (which obviously you'll have to install before doing any of the following steps shown next). The first one is the barebone core set of features, allowing you to create custom automation tasks (very similar to other tools such as Gulp and Grunt), but the latter builds on top of the first one and provides deployment-specific tasks, where you only need to configure a few properties and then you're done.

Let's look at an example of a deployment task for shipit-deploy in Listing 9-1.

Listing 9-1. Example Deployment Task Using Shipit-Deploy

```
module.exports = function (shipit) {
  require('shipit-deploy')(shipit);

  shipit.initConfig({
    default: {
      workspace: '/tmp/your-project-name',
      deployTo: '/path/to/deployment',
      repositoryUrl: 'https://github.com/user/repo.git',
      ignores: ['.git', 'node_modules'],
      keepReleases: 3,
```

---

[1]http://capistranorb.com/

```
      deleteOnRollback: false,
      key: '/path/to/key',
      shallowClone: true
    },
    staging: {
      servers: 'user@staging-server.com'
    },
    production: {
      servers: 'user@production-server.com'
    }
  });
};
```

To run the code from Listing 9-1, you save it into a file called `shipitfile.js` inside your project and simply use the following command line:

```
$ npx shipit staging deploy --- to deploy to the staging server
```

Note   The previous command is using the npx[2] cli tool, which is not directly related to shipit. This tool allows you to run binaries from different modules, checking if they're locally or globally installed.

Let's quickly go over the properties configured in the task on Table 9-3.

---

[2]See https://www.npmjs.com/package/npx

Table 9-3. *List of Properties on Deployment Task*

Property	Description
default.workspace	This is where shipit will download the code and do all the processing before deploying it to the final folder
default.deployTo	This is the destination folder on your target server.
default.repositoryUrl	This is where the code is coming from.
default.ignores	Which files to ignore during the deployment
default.keepReleases	How many releases should be kept back, in case a rollback is required
default.deleteOnRollback	Your deployment went wrong, and you need to rollback. Do you delete those no-longer-needed files? Hint: The answer is in this property.
default.key	Path to your ssh pub key. This might be optional if you have your system already configured with the default key in the right place.
default.shallowClone	This is related to the depth of the `git clone` performed. Usually it's a good idea to leave it on TRUE.
staging.servers	List of staging servers to which you want to deploy (That's right, I said servers, as in plural.)
production.servers	Same as previous option, but for production servers

For the complete list of options, please take a look at their documentation.[3]

It is important to note that Shipit will create a particular folder structure on the target server to properly manage the latest deployed version and as many as you specified in the config file (remember the keepReleases property?). You can see the folder structure in Listing 9-2.

Listing 9-2. Folder structure created by Shipit

```
/your/app/folder
|- current -> releases/20180429140211
|- releases
    |-- 20180429140211
    |-- 20180427130000
    |-- 20171231200203
```

---

[3]https://github.com/shipitjs/shipit-deploy/blob/master/README.md#options

The root folder is the one specified in the deployTo property from Table 9-3, but shipit is not just dumping the code there; instead, it's creating a new folder inside the releases one, named using the current year, month, day, hour, minutes, and seconds of the current timestamp.

The current directory is actually a symlink pointing to the latest folder created inside releases. So at first, rolling back a version is as simple as re-pointing a linux symlink. Cool, huh?

This approach is super flexible and powerful at the same time. It also simplifies other tasks, such as configuring document roots in the web server, if you were to be deploying a web app, since you'd also be setting it up to be /your/app/folder/current/public (for instance), and no matter what the current active version is, you'll always send back a response with the web server on.

Installation

Finally, to install both utilities, you can do so, like this:

```
$npm install -g shipit-cli
$npm install -g shipit-deploy
```

What about Continuous Integration?

You might be wondering, what about CI? Isn't that what this is supposed to be doing? Why do I have to manually deploy?

And you'd be right, you can definitely set up a CI server that will take care of doing this for you, but inside those automated tasks, you might end up configuring the execution of Shipit tasks.

Just so we're all on the same page, a CI server is one that can be configured to automate your deployments (usually they're language-agnostic, though they might have language-specific plug-ins). People usually hook them up to code repository triggers, so you can deploy by simply pushing into a specific branch. Some of the most common CI servers are TravisCI,[4] Jenkins,[5] and Bamboo.[6] Figure 9-5 shows an example diagram of how that interaction would look.

---

[4]https://travis-ci.org/
[5]https://jenkins.io/
[6]https://www.atlassian.com/software/bamboo

Figure 9-5. Sample interaction between your CI, a GIT repo, and your production servers

With this set-up, you configure a post-commit hook on your git repository to notify your CI environment when new code gets committed (this can also be done by configuring your CI servers to check the repo periodically, looking for changes). Once the CI tasks get triggered, your project will build, and this can mean anything, literally; it all depends on you and the steps you want to take here.

Usually during this step, you'll perform some testing tasks, such as running unit tests to make sure the code you're about to deploy actually works. This is such a common task that CI platforms usually have plugins that will detect whether the tests failed or not, to know if they can actually deploy the code or halt the deployment until you provide a fix.

The final step here would be to copy the code into the right place, and here is where shipit comes again; you could simply have it pre-installed in your CI servers (depends on the kind of access you have to them) and run your cli command using a task. If you can't install custom packages in your CI, which sometimes you can't, you can probably have it on your destination servers, and run the command remotely from your CI script. Either way, Shipit is a tool that can be used independently or as part of your continuous integration process.

PM2

Let me paint you a picture: You got your code ready, you managed to deploy it, and much to your own surprise, it's working! And minutes later, your platform is being used. You sit down, sip on your very well-deserved cup of joe (the one that reads "Best programmer in the w0r1d"—you earned it after all), and start thinking about the next big project, pondering the new challenges that lie ahead, never wanting or needing to look back at your old projects, hoping they'll live happily and joyfully without your intervention. Sounds nice, doesn't it? Yeah... It's all a lie though; you'll never get that happy ending, not unless you quit your job right after the first deployment.

Don't go getting depressed on me now; it's never going to happen, but that's normal. Nobody gets that happy ending, that is why tools such as PM2 exist. You need to monitor and maintain your processes once deployed. Well, either you or someone from another team needs to, but you get my point (usually developers don't actively monitor production systems, but they might be the ones fixing the issues in the end).

Why Do You Need a Process Manager?

You technically don't. Node.js is completely capable of functioning without one; that's not the point. The point here is that you're on a production environment, and as we've been covering during this entire chapter, failure here should not be an option, and if (and when) it happens, you need all the tools at your disposal to (a) understand why it happened, and (b) recover from it.

You can very well start your production process simply doing the good old:

```
$ sudo nohup node index.js  & ---you'd be using sudo here to allow us to
listen on port 80
```

That will work, it'll log your std.out into a nohup.out file, and thanks to nohup it won't close once you close the ssh connection to your server. But how much memory are your processes consuming? What happens if they crash due to a bug, or a lack of resources, or something else? Really, you got your process up and running, but that's as far as you'll get. This is far from ideal and a place where you generally don't want to be.

So, What Now?

Enter PM2, a process manager capable of keeping your processes alive and monitoring them at the same time. It provides a rich command line tool, web interface, and even the ability to use Node's cluster API on your processes without having to change their code.

To install it, you can simply:

```
$ npm install pm2 -g
```

After that, you can start monitoring your application by starting it with PM2 (as seen in Figure 9-6), like so (Listing 9-3 shows an actual program that we'll monitor using pm2):

```
$pm2 start index.js --name "my app" -i max
```

```
fernandodoglio@UY-IT00066 ~/workspace/personal/http-sample $ pm2 start index.js --name "my app" -i max
[PM2] Starting /home/fernandodoglio/workspace/personal/http-sample/index.js in cluster_mode (0 instance)
[PM2] Done.
```

App name	id	mode	pid	status	restart	uptime	cpu	mem	user	watching
my app	0	cluster	27226	online	0	0s	60%	33.0 MB	fernandodoglio	disabled
my app	1	cluster	27232	online	0	0s	81%	33.6 MB	fernandodoglio	disabled
my app	2	cluster	27238	online	0	0s	99%	32.1 MB	fernandodoglio	disabled
my app	3	cluster	27248	online	0	0s	80%	27.4 MB	fernandodoglio	disabled

```
Use `pm2 show <id|name>` to get more details about an app
```

Figure 9-6. *Output from the pm2 start command*

The output shown on Figure 9-6, is what you would see if you started your application on a similar system as mine. Decomposing the start command, you can see that the --name parameter is used to provide a human readable identifier that can be used to reference the entire group of processes. The -i max modifier tells PM2 to use the maximum amount of cores in your system (mine has four), so right off the bat, we're clustering the application, without having to even think about it on our code (look at Listing 9-3 as proof).

Tip   You can start your application with a pre-defined memory limit (using the --memory-max-restart [limit][M|G|K] modifier). If you do, PM2 will restart your process once it reaches that limit.

Note   All processes are now being actively monitored by PM2, and if any of them crashes for any reason, it'll be automatically restarted.

Listing 9-3. Sample Program Used on the PM2 Start Example

```
const http = require('http');

function serve(ip, port)
{
    http.createServer( (req, res)  => {
        console.log("[LOG] Request received");
```

```
        res.writeHead(200, {'Content-Type': 'text/plain'}); // Return a 200
                                                                response
        res.write(JSON.stringify(req.headers));             // Respond with
                                                                request
                                                                headers
        res.end("\nServer Address: "+ip+":"+port+"\n");     // Let us
                                                                know the
                                                                server that
                                                                responded

    }).listen(port, ip);
    console.log('Server running at http://'+ip+':'+port+'/');
}

serve('0.0.0.0', 9000);
```

Logging with console.log is not a great idea usually, because you can't really do much with the console output, but if you've decided to stick to that, PM2 captures anything thrown at stdin and stoud, so with a simple:

```
$ pm2 logs
```

you'll get the last 15 lines of logs for each process (as seen in Figure 9-7). You can also specify the id of the process for which you want to see the logs.

```
/home/fernandodoglio/.pm2/logs/my-app-out-1.log last 15 lines:
1|my app    | Server running at http://0.0.0.0:9000/

/home/fernandodoglio/.pm2/logs/my-app-out-0.log last 15 lines:
0|my app    | Server running at http://0.0.0.0:9000/

/home/fernandodoglio/.pm2/logs/my-app-out-3.log last 15 lines:
3|my app    | Server running at http://0.0.0.0:9000/

/home/fernandodoglio/.pm2/logs/my-app-out-2.log last 15 lines:
2|my app    | Server running at http://0.0.0.0:9000/
```

Figure 9-7. Output from pm2 logs

You also have your basic commands such as pm2 restart "my app" if you want to restart all your API processes. Or pm2 stop "my app" if you need the manager to stop all processes.

Another helpful command is the `pm2 monit` one, which brings up a console UI with general monitoring features. As you can see on Figure 9-8, you get a global overview of the system, with the possibility of browsing through that data using your arrow keys.

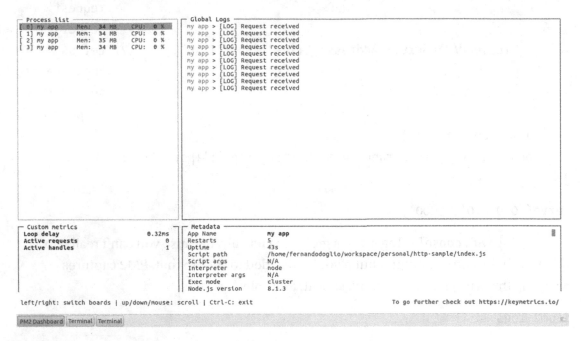

Figure 9-8. *Console UI for monitoring the current status of your processes*

The last feature I'd like to cover in this chapter (you should definitely look into the main documentation,[7] since there is quite a lot I'm leaving out) is the process metrics. With this feature, you can register a function in your code to provide a metric that can be read from PM2 monitoring UI.

Let's take a look and add a request counter to the previous code—something simple to get us started. To get this to work, you first need to install the pmx module; after that you can update the code as follows:

---

[7]http://pm2.keymetrics.io/docs/usage/quick-start/

Listing 9-4. Custom Metric Code Added to the Example

```
const http = require('http');
const Probe = require("pmx").probe();

let REQUEST_COUNTER = 0;

Probe.metric({
        name: 'request counter',
        value: () => REQUEST_COUNTER
});

function serve(ip, port)
{
    http.createServer( (req, res) => {
        console.log("[LOG] Request received");
        REQUEST_COUNTER++;
        res.writeHead(200, {'Content-Type': 'text/plain'}); // Return a 200
                                                            response

        res.write(JSON.stringify(req.headers));             // Respond with
                                                            request
                                                            headers

        res.end("\nServer Address: "+ip+":"+port+"\n");     // Let us
                                                            know the
                                                            server that
                                                            responded

    }).listen(port, ip);
    console.log('Server running at http://'+ip+':'+port+'/');
}

serve('0.0.0.0', 9000);
```

You can get the metric's value using pm2 show [ID] to get a snapshot of the entire process, or start the monitoring UI and get a real-time view of the metrics.

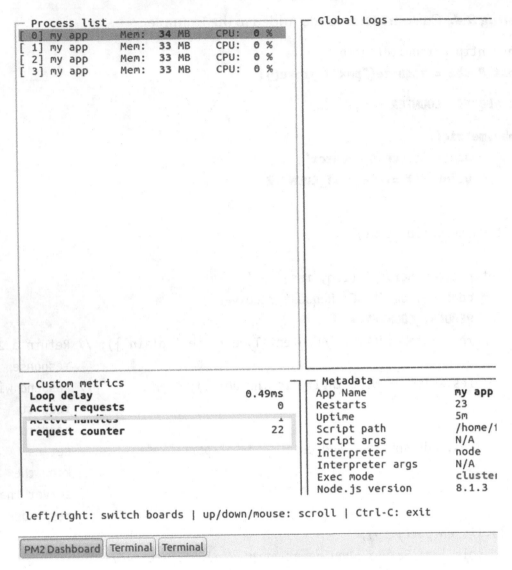

Figure 9-9. *Monitoring UI showing custom metrics values*

Summary

In this chapter, we covered the basic concepts to take into account when creating your production environment and when (and how) to promote code from one environment to the other.

In the next and final chapter, I'm going to cover some basic troubleshooting for this type of application.

CHAPTER 10

Troubleshooting

This is it. You made it to the final chapter. You experienced first-hand what it takes to write a RESTful API in Node. You've gone over the theory. You learned what REST actually stands for and how to use it to develop a good and useful API.

In this chapter, I'll cover some of the things that can go wrong during the process and some of the considerations you have to take into account, such as the following:

- Asynchronous programming: I'll take one final shot at this subject, explaining how it was used in our code.

- Minor details about the Swagger UI configuration: Sometimes the documentation is not enough.

- Potential CORS issues: I'll go over the basics of CORS to help you understand how to use it to your advantage.

- Data types: The last subject that I'll cover regarding our code is how to go from JSON Schemas data types to Mongoose types.

Asynchronous Programming

For the mind of the non-JavaScript developer, or even for the non-Node.js developer, the concept of asynchronous programming might be a strange one to grasp at first. And I say "might" because it's not a JavaScript/Node.js–unique concept; other programming languages, like Earlang, Python, and even the more recent Go have this capacity.

That being said, Node.js is one of the few environments where a web developer is kind of forced to deal with this concept or is unable to properly develop.

Asynchronous programming becomes a must on any mid-sized project using Node. js when you start dealing with external resources, mainly because that means you'll be using third-party libraries that are already taking advantage of this programming technique; so you either embrace it or switch languages.

© Fernando Doglio 2018
F. Doglio, *REST API Development with Node.js*, https://doi.org/10.1007/978-1-4842-3715-1_10

You've already covered how this feature improves the performance of applications, and you even saw a couple of useful design patterns that leverage it, so let's now discuss how failing to grasp this concept could hurt your understanding of the code presented in Chapter 7.

Whether or not you've noticed, in our API's code, there are several places where asynchronous programming takes place. Let's look at some of them.

The Controllers Action's Code

Every action on every controller has a piece of asynchronous programming in the form of database queries. This is probably the most obvious bit, but it's important to go over it to understand it properly.

The reason why we don't do anything like Listing 10-1.

Listing 10-1. Example of a Database Query Inside One of Our Controllers (authors.js file)

```
var authors = lib.db.model('Author')
    .find(criteria).exec()

if(!authors) return next(controller.RESTError('InternalServerError',
authors))
controller.writeHAL(res, authors)
```

And instead, we set up a call-back function, like shown in Listing 10-1:

```
lib.db.model('Author')
            .find(criteria)
            .exec((err, authors) => {
                    if(err) return next(controller.RESTError
                    ('InternalServerError', err))
                    controller.writeHAL(res, authors)
            })
```

This is because, as I've already stated, I/O operations in Node.js are *asynchronous*, which means that querying the database needs to be done like this, with a call-back function set up to handle the response once it arrives. It is true that Node.js provides synchronous versions of its I/O functions (like reading and writing files), but they're mostly there to simplify the transition; you're not being encouraged to use them, and third-party libraries like Mongoose aren't interested in following that pattern either.

Catching this type of error while manually testing your application might be a bit of a headache, because the resulting behavior might not always be the same. When the code is complex enough, it becomes a race between the time it takes for the asynchronous function to get a response back and the time it takes for your code to use that value.

Also, because the Node.js interpreter won't throw an error if you miss some of the parameters on a method/function call, you might end up doing something like that in Listing 10-2.

Listing 10-2. Sample Code Showing Missing Attributes

```
const fs = require("fs");

function libraryMethod(attr1, callback) {
 fs.readFile(attr1, function(err, response){
    if(callback) callback(response)
 })
}
var returnValue = libraryMethod('index.js')
```

The code from Listing 10-2 will not throw an error—ever. And you'll always get undefined in your returnValue. And if you don't have access to the code of the libraryMethod function, it might be difficult to understand what's wrong.

For instance, you have a code like in Listing 10-3.

Listing 10-3. Example of an Incorrect Asynchronous Code that Works Correctly Sometimes

```
const fs = require("fs");
const request = require("request");

let myResponseValue = ''
fs.readFile('./yourfile.txt', (err, response) => {
   myResponseValue = response
})
```

```
//The time for the following request might vary, and the results with it
request.get('http://www.google.com', () => {
    console.log(myResponseValue)
})
```

Listing 10-3 shows another common mistake when working with asynchronous calls: you properly set up the call-back, but you used the returned value outside of that callback.

In the preceding example, if the `readFile` call takes less than the request to Google to get a response, it'll work, but you won't realize your mistake until something happens (such as the code going to production). Suddenly, `readFile` is reading a larger file than expected, thus taking longer to finish, and now an empty string is always printing to the console. But you don't know why, of course. The simple way to fix this is to add any code dealing with the response value *inside* the callback function.

The Middleware Functions

This might not be obvious at first glance, but the entire middleware chain is following the serial flow mechanics mentioned back in Chapter 3. How can you tell? Because of the next function; you need to call it when the function is over and ready to give control to the next middleware.

You can have even more asynchronous code inside the function and still be able to call the next function, thanks to `next`.

In some places this isn't really visible, like when setting up the `queryParser` and `bodyParser` middleware:

```
server.use(restify.plugins.queryParser())
server.use(restify.plugins.bodyParser())
```

But those methods are actually returning a new function, which in turn receives the three magic parameters: the request object, the response object, and the next function.

A common issue when creating custom middleware is forgetting to call the `next` function (see Listing 10-4 for an example) in one of the possible execution branches of your code (if you happen to have them). Symptoms of this are that your API appears to hang up, you never get a response back from the server, and you don't see any errors on the console. This is due to the fact that the execution flow is broken. Suddenly it's unable to find a way to continue, and you're not sending back a response (using the response object).

This is tricky to catch, since there aren't any error messages to clearly state the problem.

Listing 10-4. Example of an Ill-constructed Middleware Function

```
function middleware(req, res, next){
  if(req.params.q == '1') {
     next()
  } else {
    if(req.params.q2 == '1') {
       next()
    }
  }
}
```

Looking at Listing 10-4 we can infer that if no "q" or "q2" parameters are sent, or if they don't have the right values, then this middleware function is breaking the serial flow and no response is ever getting back to the client.

There is another type of middleware used on the project: Mongoose middleware, which are the hooks you can attach to models to be executed before or after a set of specific actions. Our particular case used a post-save hook on the clientreview model, see Listing 10-5 for an example.

Listing 10-5. Sample Middleware Function Used with MongooseJS

```
modelDef.schema.post('save', function(doc, next) {
        db.model('Book').update({_id: doc.book}, {$addToSet: {reviews:
        this.id}}, next
)
  })
```

This code clearly shows the next function being used in conjunction with an asynchronous call inside the middleware. If you were to forget to call next, then the execution would be interrupted (and halted) at this call-back.

Issues Configuring the Swagger UI

Setting up the Swagger UI is a task that requires both a change to the UI itself and some special code on the back end. This is not particularly easy to understand since the documentation is not exactly simple to read.

On the one hand, we're using the swagger-node-restify module to generate the back-end endpoints needed by the UI; this is achieved in the following lines in the index.js file from Chapter 7:

1. `swagger.addModels(lib.schemas)`

2. `swagger.setAppHandler(server)`

3. `lib.helpers.setupRoutes(server, swagger, lib)`

4. `swagger.configureSwaggerPaths("", "/api-docs", "")`

5. `swagger.configure('http://localhost:9000', '0.1')`

Line 1 sets up the models, so that Swagger can return them when the endpoints specify them as the response class. Line 2 is basically telling the module which web server we are using for the documentation. We could potentially have two different servers configured: one for the documentation and one for the actual API.

Line 3 is actually one of ours, but it does require Swagger, because we're calling the `addGET`, `addPOST`, `addDELETE`, or `addPUT` methods provided by it. This is done by the `BaseController` code in its `setUpActions` method, with the code from Listing 10-6.

Listing 10-6. Snippet from Chapter 7 Showing Where We Deal with Swagger's Methods

```
this.actions.forEach(act => {
        let method = act['spec']['method']
        logger.info(`Setting up auto-doc for (${method} ) - ${act['spec']
        ['nickname']}`)
        sw['add' + method](act)
        app[method.toLowerCase()](act['spec']['path'], act['action'])
}).
```

Line 4 doesn't really say much, but it's useful for several reasons:

- The most obvious one is that we're setting up the path for the documentation: /api-docs.

- We're also saying that we don't want to specify formats via extension (i.e., .json). By default, we need to define a {format} section in our path to be autoreplaced by .json. With this specific line, we're removing the need for that and simplifying the path formats.

Finally, line 5 sets the base URL for the entire documentation API.

In Chapter 7, the front-end code had to change; I mentioned where exactly. Uncommenting the code for the API key and the change in the host URL are obviously needed, but the change in the resource path isn't. We need to change this because of the way we configured the static path during the initialization phase (check Listing 10-7 for more details).

Listing 10-7. Code Used to Set Up the Static Route to Return Swagger's UI

```
server.get(/^\/swagger-ui(\/.*)?/, restifyPlugins.serveStatic({
            directory: __dirname + '/',
            default: 'index.html'
    }))
```

Note   The code from Listing 10-7 uses the special variable __dirname, which even though we've not defined, is already available and contains the current working directory of the executed script.

The code from Listing 10-7 ensures that only anything under the swagger-ui folder is served as static content (which is basically everything that the Swagger UI needs), but the default path that comes in the HTML file points to the root folder, which isn't good enough in our case.

CORS: a.k.a. Cross-Origin Resource Sharing

Any web developer who's been at it for a while has seen this dreaded error message:

XMLHttpRequest cannot load http://domain.example. Origin http://domain1.example is not allowed by Access-Control-Allow-Origin.

For developers working on a web client for a public API, the browser checks for *cross-origin resource sharing* (CORS) to make sure that the request is secure, which means that the browser checked the requested endpoint and since it's not finding any CORS headers, or the headers don't specify our domain as valid, it is cancelling the request for security reasons.

For API designers, this is a very relevant error because CORS needs to be taken into account, either by manually allowing it or by denying it.

If you're designing a public API, you need to make sure that you specify in the response headers that any domain can make a request. This is the most permissive of all possible settings.

If, on the other hand, you're defining a private API, then the CORS headers help define the only domains that can actually request any kind of resource of the endpoints.

Normally, a web client will follow a set of steps on every CORS request:

1. First, the client will ask the API server if the desired request is possible (Can the client query the wanted resource using the needed method from the current origin?). This is done by sending a "pre-flight"[1] request with the Access-Control-Request-Header header (with the headers the client needs to access) and the Access-Control-Request-Method header (with the method needed).

2. Then the server will answer with what is authorized, using these headers: Access-Control-Allow-Origin with the allowed origin (or * for anything), Access-Control-Allowed-Methods with the valid methods, and Access-Control-Allow-Headers with a list of valid headers to be sent.

3. Finally, the client can do the "normal" request.

---

[1]An OPTIONS request.

If anything fails to validate during the pre-flight request (either the requested method or the headers needed), then the response will not be a 200 OK response.

For our case, according to the code in Chapter 7, we're going for the public API approach, since we're allowing any domains to do requests to our endpoints with the code in the index.js file shown in Listing 10-8:

Listing 10-8. Example Code Used to Set the CORS Headers on Every Endpoint of Our API Data Types

```
restify.defaultResponseHeaders = data => {
        this.header('Access-Control-Allow-Origin', '*')
    }
```

Even though we're not directly handling and specifying types for our variables throughout the API's JavaScript code, there are two very specific places where data types are needed: the JSON Schemas defined for our resources and the Mongoose models defined.

Now, thanks to the code in the `getModelFromSchema` function and the `translateTypeToJs` function, you can go from JSON Schema types to Mongoose types because most of the basic types defined in our schemas are almost directly translatable into JavaScript types.

For the more complex types, like arrays, since the entire definition is different, extra code needs to be added, which is where the `getModelFromSchema` code comes in.

The type's translation from the code in Chapter 7 is limited to what was needed at the time, but you could easily extend it to achieve further functionalities, like getting the `required` attribute to work for both the schema validator and the Mongoose validators (these make sure you don't save anything invalid). Let's quickly look at how to go about adding support for the `required` property.

An *object* type is composed of a series of properties but also a list of required properties, which is defined at the same level as the `properties` attribute. Take a look at Listing 10-9 for an example of that:

Listing 10-9. Example Showing how to Set Two Attributes (Name and Website) as "Required" in the JSON Schema

```
module.exports = {
    "id": "Author",
    "properties": {
        "name": {
```

```
            "type": "string",
            "description": "The full name of the author"
        },
    "description": {
            "type": "string",
            "description": "A small bio of the author"
        },
    "books": {
            "type": "array",
            "description": "The list of books published on at least one of
                            the stores by this author",
            "items": {
                "$ref": "Book"
            }
        },
    "website": {
            "type": "string",
            "description": "The Website url of the author"
        },
    "avatar": {
            "type": "string",
            "description": "The url for the avatar of this author"
        },
    "address": {
            "type": "object",
            "properties": {
                "street": {
                    "type": "string"
                },
                "house_number": {
                    "type": "integer"
                }
            }
        }
```

```
        }
    },
    "required": ["name", "website"]
}
```

To get the content of this new property, you just need to add a few lines to the getModelFromSchema function to simply check for the property name; and if it's inside the required array, you set it as required. See Listing 10-10 for more details.

Listing 10-10. Single Line Added to the Function (Inside lib/db.js File) to Allow Support for Required Attributes

```
function getModelFromSchema(schema) {
        let data = {
                name: schema.id,
                schema: {}
        }

        let newSchema = {}
        let tmp = null
        _.each(schema.properties, (v, propName) => {
        v.required = schema.required && schema.required.indexOf(propName)
        != -1;
                if(v['$ref'] != null) {
                        tmp = {
                                type: Schema.Types.ObjectId,
                                ref: v['$ref']
                        }
                } else {
                        tmp = translateComplexType(v)
                }
                newSchema[propName] = tmp
        })

        data.schema = new Schema(newSchema)
        return data
}
```

Summary

This is it. You made it. And you managed to go through the entire book! You went from the basics of REST to a full-blown RESTful API. Finally, in this chapter, you learned the main things that can cause trouble during the development process, such as asynchronous programming, configuring the Swagger UI, CORS, and moving from JSON Schema types to Mongoose types.

Thank you for reading and, hopefully, enjoying the book.

Index

A

addAction method, 200, 244
API design
  description, 39
  Developer eXperience (DX)
    access points, 41–42
    communication protocol, 40–41
    uniform interface, 42–45
  error handling
    client development stage, 53–55
    end users, 55–56
  extensibility
    Chromium project, 48
    Facebook APIs, 46
    Google APIs, 46
    Semantic Versioning, 49
    Twitter APIs, 46
    versioning scheme, 49
    versions of API, 46–48
  scalability
    bookstore, 69
    distributed architecture, 68–69
    entities, 69
    estimation, 66
    monolithic architecture, 66–67
  SDK/libraries, 56–57
  security
    authentication, 57
    authorization, 57
    Basic Auth, TSL, 58–59

    Digest Auth, 60–61
    MAC signing process, 65
    OAuth 1.0a, 62–63
    OAuth 2.0, 64
    RESTful systems, 57
    stateless methods, 58, 64–65
  up-to-date documentation
    4chan's API
      documentation, 51–52
    Facebook's developer site, 51
    Mashape service, 50
    optional parameters, 50
    success/failure reasons, 52
api_key parameter, 193
Asynchronous programming
  benefits, 74
  callback function, 72
  controllers action's code, 304–306
  error reports, 75
  execution flow, 74
  instructions, 73
  I/O operation, 81–84
  middleware functions, 306–307
  Node.js, 303
  parallel function, 76–79
  serial flow, 79–80
  simple file read operation, 75–76

B

body parser, 258

315

© Fernando Doglio 2018
F. Doglio, *REST API Development with Node.js*, https://doi.org/10.1007/978-1-4842-3715-1

W

Web Service
  Description Language
  (WSDL), 32–35
writeHAL
  method, 200, 281

X, Y, Z

XML-RPC
  architecture, 29–30
  request, 28–29
  response, 29
  SOAP, 36